Read It! Play It!

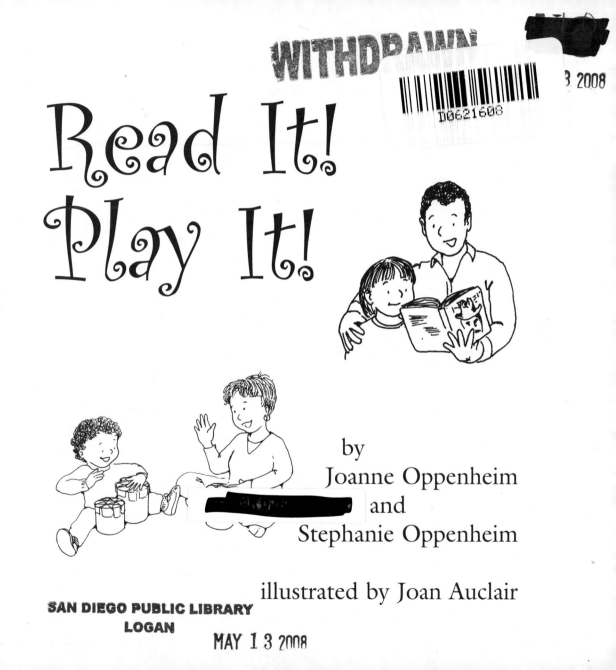

by
Joanne Oppenheim
and
Stephanie Oppenheim

illustrated by Joan Auclair

Acknowledgment

The core idea of the Read It! Play It!™ Literacy Initiative is to instill the message that reading can be a lifelong source of pleasure. To help us reach as many families as possible, we are grateful to Reading Is Fundamental™, the nation's leading children's literacy organization. RIF will distribute thousands of copies of Read It! Play It!™ to their literacy programs across America. Reading Is Fundamental™ will also receive a $1 from every copy of the book we sell.

We would also like to acknowledge the generous contributions of our corporate sponsors, LeapFrog™ and Toys "R" Us.™ Their support is making the contributions to RIF possible and enabling us to reach a broader audience. Perhaps most gratifying is that both companies share our commitment to literacy, learning, and play.

This book may be purchased for educational, business, or sales promotional use. For information contact: Stephanie Oppenheim, Publisher, Oppenheim Toy Portfolio, Inc., 40 East 9th St., Suite 14M, New York, NY 10003, or call (212) 598-0502, or e-mail stephanie@toyportfolio.com.

Designed by Joan Auclair

ISBN: 09721050-1-8

Reading Is Fundamental™, Inc., prepares and motivates children to read by delivering free books and literacy resources to those children and families who need them most. The oldest and largest non-profit children's and family literacy organization in the United States, RIF operates through a network of 450,000 volunteers—from teachers to parents, librarians to caregivers—and gives away 16.5 million books a year to over five million children at more than 25,000 sites nationwide.

You can find RIF in schools, libraries, community centers, childcare centers, hospitals, migrant worker camps, Head Start and Even Start programs, homeless shelters, and detention centers. Our priority is reaching children who are most at risk of educational failure with reading motivation activities and the excitement of choosing free books to keep. We encourage family and community involvement through a wide range of literacy training and resources.

Since our founding in 1966, RIF has provided more than 265 million books for children to choose and keep, thanks to the generous support of the U.S. Department of Education, corporations, foundations, community organizations, and thousands of individuals. To support RIF's work or to learn about volunteer opportunities, please visit ***www.rif.org*** and click on "How you can help."

LeapFrog™ Enterprises, Inc. is proud to support the Oppenheim Toy Portfolio's Read It! Play It!™ Literacy Initiative in our joint effort to help children Learn Something New Every Day.™

LeapFrog™ is totally committed to creating engaging, effective learning experiences that inspire and delight kids by developing innovative products for use at home, in schools and around the world. At LeapFrog™, every teacher and technician, every engineer and artist, everyone here puts learning first. This philosophy fuels the entire company.

Our highly specialized teams put the crucial, creative elements together to make learning feel like magic. They understand how to intellectually captivate and emotionally engage the minds and imaginations of children turning obstacles into opportunities, challenges into triumphs.

LeapFrog™ knows that learning is not a part-time commitment. It requires a tremendous amount from every member of our team. We are passionately devoted to delighting and engaging children in a meaningful way that will inspire a lifelong love of learning. Our future is in the hands of our children and they deserve our best—every day.

The Toys "R" Us™ Children's Fund, Inc.

Established in 1992, The Toys "R" Us™ Children's Fund, Inc. has been committed to funding charities and organizations that benefit children's health and well-being. Thanks to the ongoing dedication of associates from Toys "R" Us™, Inc. and the many suppliers, vendors, sponsors and friends who so generously donate every year, The Fund is making a wonderful difference in the lives of children in need. This year, we are proud to continue to expand our highly successful signature programs. The major focus of The Children's Fund is two important initiatives, literacy and kid's playrooms. Toys "R" Us™ has been fortunate to form some very special partnerships in an effort to develop these important programs. Along with our own signature reading program, Reading Ready: Preparing Children to be Lifelong Readers, The Fund has partnered with Reading Is Fundamental: Family of Readers™. These programs give kids the tools they need to become enthusiastic and devoted readers.

Sharing books with children is more than a pleasurable way of spending time together. It is one of the most significant ways of leading children to an early delight in books and reading. It's no secret that children who are read to frequently during their early years tend to become better readers, with greater ease, during their early school years. Nor should it be surprising that children's vocabulary and language skills are greatly enhanced by their experiences with storybooks.

The "Play It!" ideas can expand the pleasures found in reading. Along with the long-term academic benefits, sharing books with children can provide more immediate payoffs.

- Well-chosen storybooks spark lively discussions, fuel creative thinking, and inspire active play.
- Through books we can share the excitement and suspense of an adventure and the pleasure of happily-ever-afters.
- Books enlarge your children's world, with information that helps them understand how things work.
- Stories can reflect children's feelings and provide them with the comfort of knowing that others have felt as they do.
- Books provide adults and children a common departure gate where together they can journey to worlds beyond their everyday experiences.

Why these books?

All the books selected are developmentally appropriate for the preschool and early school years. Some are classics you may have enjoyed as a child; several others are relatively new titles that we hope will become classics! We have also selected books that are widely available in bookstores and libraries. **Keep in mind** that while many of the activities promote independent play, those that include cooking, cutting, or sharp utensils will require adult supervision.

Happy Reading & Playing!

Leading to Reading: A Dozen Building Blocks for Literacy

Becoming literate begins long before children start to school. From the time they are old enough to enjoy the little rhymes you say or point to a picture on the printed page children begin the process of becoming readers. Reading aloud to children is key to establishing connections to books and reading. Beyond the warmth of sharing books, here are 12 easy ways to build their literacy skills:

1. **Share your pleasure in reading.** As you read with expression, even hamming it up and using many voices, children "read" your obvious pleasure in reading and books. Building that pleasure connection to books is key to fostering your children's love of books.
2. **Demystify how books work.** In reading a book from front to back, from left to right, you are demonstrating in a concrete way how books "work." Children do not automatically know that the little black squiggles on the page are the words we speak. Occasionally, move your hand under the words you read to help them see how the words go from left to right.
3. **Predict what will happen next.** As you are reading a story, pause from time to time to ask, "What do you think will happen next?" There's no right or wrong answer, but making predictions develops children's sense of story.
4. **Talk about the story.** When you pause, encourage children to look at the illustrations for story clues or talk about the playful language or ways the artist has shown some part of the story.
5. **Let the illustrations speak.** When children use the illustrations to "re-read" a story they have heard, they are developing their comprehension and language skills.
6. **Share the telling.** Involve your child in the telling of the story. Many stories have repeated refrains that children love to say. Pause in your reading, giving them a chance to chime in with, "I think I can, I think I can."

7. **Retell a tale.** Retelling a story calls for children to recall the sequence of events and put the story in their own words—a first step to writing.
8. **Take cues from your child's interests.** Select books that relate to your child's interests or experiences. A preschooler who is engrossed in dinosaurs or transportation will relish books that provide an opportunity to learn more. You may not be able to stay at the firehouse for hours, but a book about firetrucks can be pored over whenever the child desires.
9. **Books of their own.** Building a library of books that a child can return to again and again is very satisfying way of building book connections. It gives them a sense of ownership in the pleasure of books. Unlike adults who usually read a book once and move on, children gain new things with each reading. One time they may listen for the pleasure of the story; another reading may build their excitement with the words or the bigger idea that most good storybooks have at their heart.
10. **Keep reading—even to readers.** Continue to read to early school-age children, even if they are reading independently. Beginning readers can understand books that are far more complex than the books they can read on their own.
11. **Extend a story through play.** Enjoy activities that extend the books you share—cooking, art activities, science, role-play can make book connections come alive in new ways.
12. **Reading and writing go hand in hand.** Encourage your child to retell some of these stories in his or her own words. In turning the pages of the book and "reading" the pictures or remembering the sequence of a well loved story such as *The Three Bears* or *The Story of Ping,* your child is gaining a sense that stories have a beginning, middle, and end. Recalling the sequence of events and putting them in their own words is a huge step toward building the underpinnings for reading comprehension.

TABLE OF CONTENTS

TABLE OF CONTENTS

ART

MATH

TABLE OF CONTENTS

SCIENCE/KITCHEN SCIENCE

MINES
NE
MIN
MINE

Read It!

Alphabet Mystery

(by Audrey Wood/illus. by Bruce Wood, Scholastic) All of the lowercase letters are ready to go to sleep when they discover that "x" is missing! And where can he be? Silly "x" has run away, since he is used so infrequently. When the others find him, he is with big "M," a mean, monstrous letter who threatens to make alphabet soup with the other letters. An imaginative mystery for children who are playing with and learning their letters. This is no ordinary ABC. In fact, the lowercase letters are all too often ignored in children's books. Yet these are the very letters children need to learn before they can read. 4–7. For a more traditional approach, bring home *ABC: A Child's First Alphabet Book*, by Alison Jay (Dutton), which deals with letter and sound connections.

Play It!

Sort-a-Sound Game — Phonics

Gather together a collection of small toys and household items that begin with the same two or three sounds. Start with sounds that are distinctly different from each other. For example, start with **Mm / Cc/ Pp.** The toy box, drawers, and kitchen will turn up a goodly supply of miniature cars, whistles, trucks, cows, and buttons that can be sorted into big coffee cans or plastic bowls. Involve kids in finding the objects. You can also use pictures cut out of magazines and pasted on cards to play this game.

You'll need:

- Found objects (above)—three to five objects for each sound.

- Two or three containers, each labeled with a different letter.

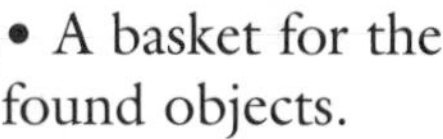

- A basket for the found objects.

Before they play, talk about the objects in the basket. Be sure your child knows what each object is called. Now it's time to decide—where will the pig go? Your child sorts the objects by their initial sounds. Once they can sort three sounds, add new cans and objects for more sounds. Kids love handling the multiple pieces of this homemade game and using their budding sense of the sounds letters say.

Rainbow Letters — Writing

Make multi-colored letters with crayons or chalk. First, you write a single letter in one color. Your child traces your letter in another color, then you trace it again in another color. A fun way to get the feel of how to write the letters.

Letter Charades — Active Play

One player uses his whole body to stand in the shape of a letter... others try to guess the letter. This whole-body approach produces some mighty creative letter making!

WHAT THEY LEARN. All of these games provide playful ways to develop phonics, prereading, and writing skills.

Read It!

Adelita: A Mexican Cinderella

(by Tomie dePaola, Putnam) There is no glass slipper in this Cinderella story, but rather a gaily embroidered shawl that provides the link to Adelita's past, present, and happily-ever-after future. This Cinderella plays a far more active role in her fate than in the traditional telling. She is a more powerful young woman for our time. As always, Tomie dePaola's art is *muy hermosa!* 6 & up.

Same & Different — Language

Talk about the ways that this version of Cinderella is the same as the original, and how it is different. It's interesting to introduce this kind of comparative literature to young children. You can do this by reading still more Cinderella stories from other cultures such as *The Korean Cinderella* (by Shirley Climo/illus. by Ruth Heller), and even encourage children to weave their own version of the tale.

Play It!

Ojos de Diós — Art

In Mexico these brightly colored "Eyes of God" are thought to bring good luck. Some are big as a window; others are small as a notepad. They are displayed especially in October during the festival of the Green Squash. Make yours big or small—and we wish you good luck!

Here's all you need:

- an assortment of different colored knitting yarn
- two straight twigs

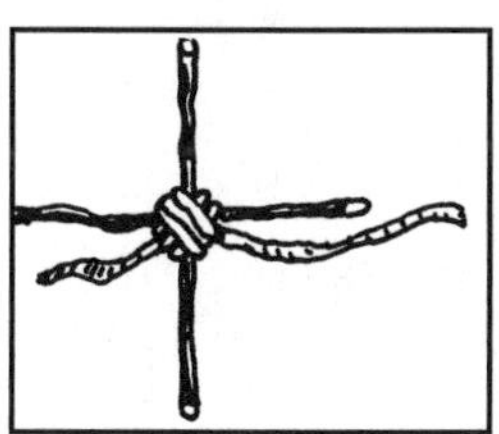

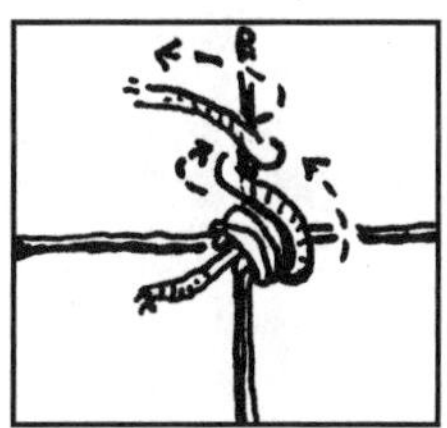

Step 1. Make a cross with the twigs and wind the yarn diagonally across the right and then the left until the twig are held together.

Step 2. Now take the yarn from behind and wrap it around the front of two spokes of the cross, wrap it around the second spoke and then wrap the yarn across the front of the next two spokes and wrap it again around the second spoke.

Step 3. When you have gone around one complete time the yarn will have formed a diamond shape.

Step 4. Continue making the diamond larger and add different colors as you go along. Try to tie the new colors onto the back so the knots will not show. Make your design as large as you like.

Step 5. Tie off the last knot as close to the spokes as you can. Add a piece of yarn to the back to hang your *ojo de diós.*

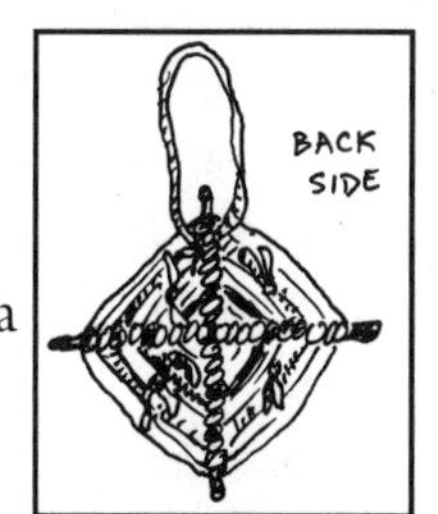

WHAT THEY LEARN. This weaving project introduces children to the art of another culture as it develops fine motor skills and memory. Once they get the knack, the craft also provides an artistic outlet for making colorful combinations with a decorative payoff.

Read It!

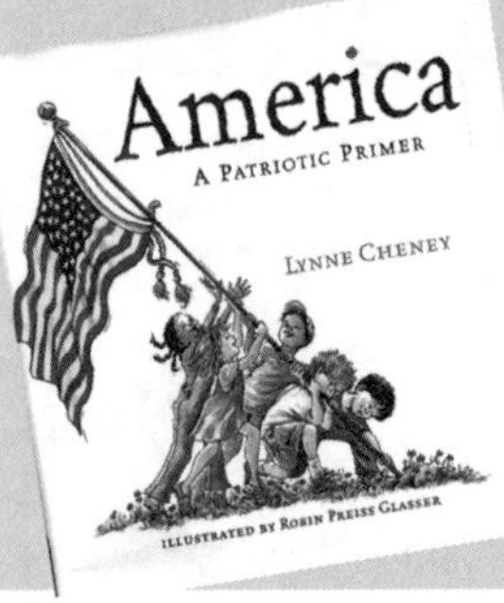

America: A Patriotic Primer

(by Lynne V. Cheney/illus. by Robin P. Glasser, Simon & Schuster) An ABC that celebrates some very important names—such as J for Jefferson and K for King, as in Martin Luther King Jr.—and some very big concepts—such as E for equality and F for freedom. Many of the ideas here will go over the heads of the younger children, but Glasser's detailed illustrations lend themselves to lots of talking along with the big ideas Cheney introduces. 6–9.

Play It!

Mark a Map — Language

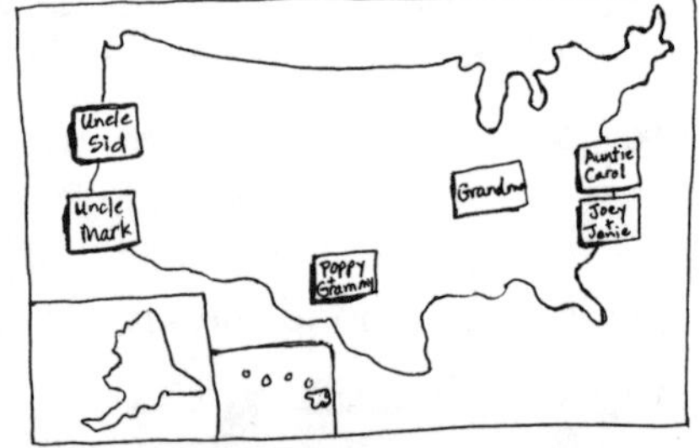

Get a map of the USA and mark all the states where members of your family live or have lived in or visited in the past. Connecting people and places gives maps more meaning for beginners.

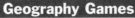

Geography Games

We can think of no geography game that's better while you are in the car or waiting for food to come in a restaurant than this classic. One of our "best" players loves to find places that end with Y so that the next player has to come up with a location that starts with a Y—not so easy. Just

in case you've forgotten, players name a city, town, state or body of water and the next player must use the last letter as the first letter of a new location.

Variation: Sports Geography

Name a city and the next player must name a team from that city.

Celebration Cake — Kitchen Science

For any patriotic occasion, a red, white, and blue flag cake is fairly easy to make, festive, and delicious, too. You'll need whipped cream, strawberries, blueberries, and a sheet cake. You can bake a cake from scratch or use a mix baked in a low oblong cake pan or brownie pan. Cover the cake with whipped cream, add a field of blue where the stars would go, and make strips of strawberries alternating with whipped cream.

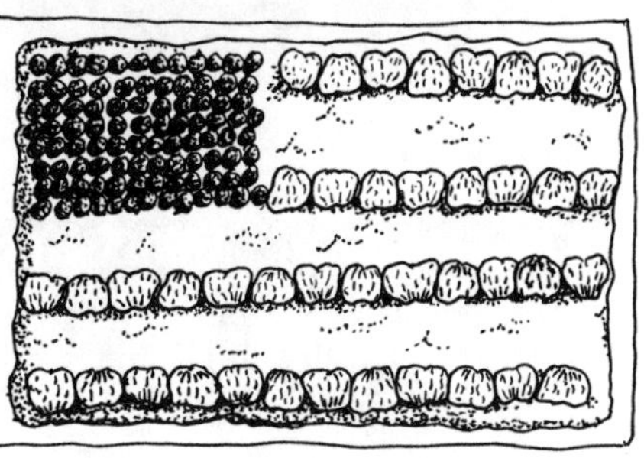

Facts of Three Game — Language

How many sets of three can your family name?

Three states on the Pacific?

Three states on the Atlantic?

Three states east of the Mississippi? west of the Mississippi?

Three land-locked states?

Three states that start with the letter M? N? W? I?

WHAT THEY LEARN.
Geography can be fun!

Read It!

Caps for Sale

(by Esphyr Slobodkina, HarperCollins) What happens when an old peddler falls asleep and a tree full of playful monkeys take his stack of hats? Kids love knowing where the hats are long before the peddler figures it out. With a repetitive refrain and humor, this has been a favorite read-aloud for generations. 3–7.

Play It!

Monkey Says! Monkey Do! **Active Play**

Talk about how the monkeys in the story were copy cats. They copied whatever the peddler did. That's how he got his caps back. Now you're going to play a copy cat game that's a lot like "Simon Says." Tell your child to listen very, very carefully! She should do only what the monkey says to do!

Step 1. Call out commands such as, "Monkey says, 'Scratch your tummy!'" Do this as you say it.

Step 2. Continue to give and act out commands.

Step 3. Say, "Touch the ground," or, "Scratch your ear," without saying, "Monkey says." If she scratches, she's out!

WHAT THEY LEARN. We often ask young children to show us "your nose, your eyes, your ears." But we sometimes forget to give them the language for less well-known body parts such as neck, shoulder, elbow, wrist, ankle, waist, palm, cheek, and chin. This game gives you a chance to build their language through play. This is an active way to help kids develop auditory memory skills as well as to build vocabulary of knowing and naming body parts.

Variation: Mirrors Game

Instead of listening, this game calls for careful looking: Player One faces Player Two, who pretends to be a mirror. Player Two, the mirror, must follow every little move that Player One makes. No talking permitted. Start with very clear movements that are easy to follow. Gradually make them more complex. Once Player Two gets the idea, switch roles and let your partner be the mirror.

Sorting Stack Game — Matching

Reread the story on a day when you are doing a big load of laundry. Remind your child of how the peddler had all the hats that looked alike in stacks. Explain that when we do the laundry, that's what we have to do. Have your child help make matching stacks of socks or towels or underwear that are the same size and color.

WHAT THEY LEARN. Sorting and matching are important skills needed for reading and math.

Read It!

Chicka Chicka Boom Boom

(by John Archambault, Bill Martin Jr./illus. Lois Ehlert, Simon & Schuster) Children love chanting the rhythmic rhyme of this alphabet book long before they understand what letters are about. This syncopated race between all the letters of the alphabet to the top of the coconut tree is a visual treat with a lively beat! Although the book is available in a sturdy boardbook format, we suggest the original text, which includes the uppercase letters that come to the rescue of those little lowercase letters that go boom, boom! 3–6.

Play It!

Chicka Chicka Go Boom Boom Game — Active Play

Tell players you are going to say several words that begin with the same sound. While you say them they should stamp their feet. But when you say one word that doesn't start with the same sound, they must "go boom, boom" and fall down. Start by saying "monkey, mouse, milk, many, man—cat." Children will stamp until you say, "cat," at which point they fall to the ground. A fun game that involves moving, listening, and a chance to be silly. **Variation:** Play a rhyming word game: "I'll say words that rhyme, such as 'hug,' 'rug,' 'bug,' 'lug,' but when I say a word that doesn't rhyme, you must go boom boom and fall down!"

Letter & Sound Detector Games

Pretend to turn on your child's "letter detector." Choose one letter that you and your child will hunt for today. If it's Monday, maybe you will hunt for MMMMMs, or how about hunting for the first letter in your child's name? Preschoolers love looking for details on signs, in books and magazines, on boxes and cans. How many Ms can you find? Be sure to stress the sound the letter says. Knowing a letter by name is not as important as learning its sounds. Add a letter on another day and play the game with both letters.

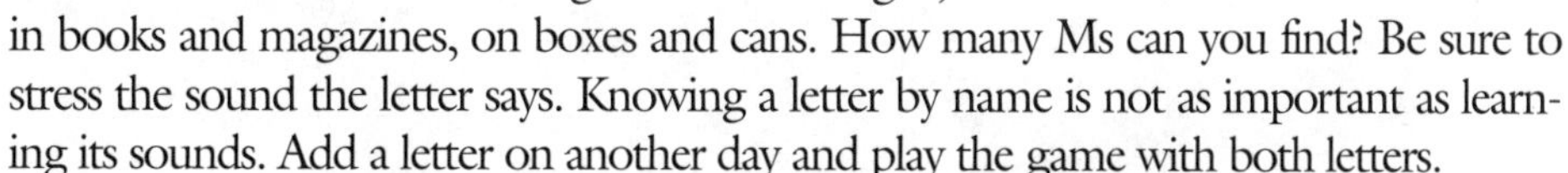

Riddle Game — Language

Pretend to switch on your "sound detector." Now say to your child, "I see something that is right in this room. It starts with the same sound as 'belt,' 'bus,' and 'bear.' Child looks until she finds a... ball, or whatever. Give extra clues as needed. Switch roles. Learning how to give riddles without saying the word take practice.

Alphabet Library: Becky's or Ben's Book of B's — Phonics

Kids love to cut and paste and make their own letter books. Instead of trying to do all the letters in one book, make a book for each letter. Finding a bunch of things that begin with the same sound is often easier and has greater value in reinforcing and learning that sound. Start with a blank book made with colored construction paper covers and four or five sheets of blank paper inside. Label it "Sara's Big Book of Bs" or "...Cs." A supply of magazines, safety scissors, and white glue will do the job. Once the pictures are in place, have your child tell you what to print under the photo. Keep the labels simple so they can "read" the books they have made. Make books for each letter and gradually your child will have a unique Alphabet Library.

Read It!

Goin' Someplace Special

(by Patricia C. McKissack/illus. by Jerry Pinkney, Atheneum) 'Tricia Ann's grandmother allows her to go downtown alone to her someplace special—a place where everyone is welcome. But getting there is not easy in the Jim Crow South, when people of color could not sit where they pleased on a bus or a park bench, in the movies, or at a restaurant. What was the one special place in Nashville where those rules were overruled? The public library! 6–9.

Talk About It!

Goin' Someplace Special is a fine story. It's also through stories that we can give children a budding sense of history. In this instance, it's a story about rights that were hard won. Here are some ideas to think and talk about: How do you suppose it would feel not to be able to sit wherever you pleased on a bus? What if you could not go into any restaurant or movie? Suppose that kind of law existed and all 7 or 8 year-old children could not eat in the cafeteria. Would that be fair? What's wrong with lumping people together and making rules that exclude them?

How Do You Get to Your Someplace Special?

Knowing how to get to her special place took Tricia Ann's courage, but she also had to know the way. Talk about the "someplace special" your child would like to get to. Is it the library? A friend's house? A store that has something special?

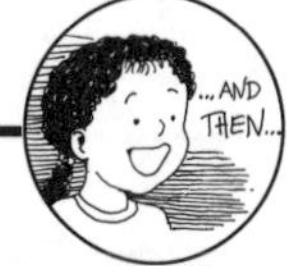

- Have him draw a picture of that special place first.
- Have him write or tell how to get to his someplace special as if he were explaining it to an alien from outer space.
- What kind of transportation will he need to take?
- Is this the fastest way?

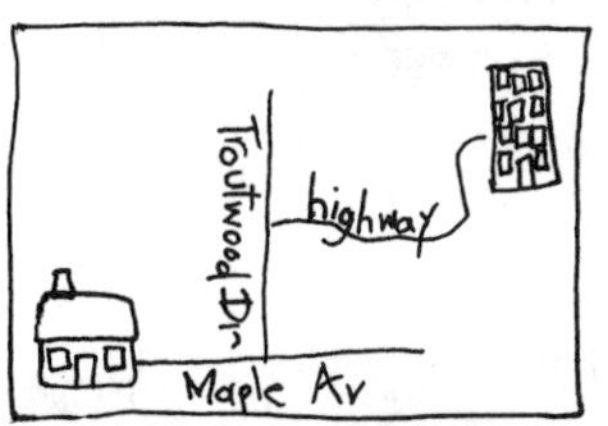

- Is there another way to go?
- Drawing a map may help him explain how to get from point A to Point B.

WHAT THEY LEARN. Kids are often eager for the independence of going places on their own. Playing this little game helps them explain the sequence of getting to an objective in their own words. Being able to explain such seemingly simple steps is not as easy as it may appear.

Sign On!

Take a trip to your public library and have your child sign on for a library card. Give your kids the library habit from the start and introduce them to the riches that await them. They'll be amazed at the variety of things they can borrow at the library as well as the number of interesting programs most public libraries have to offer.

Read It!

If a Bus Could Talk

(by Faith Ringgold, Simon & Schuster) Magic buses are not new to children's books, but this one talks and tells a young rider about a girl who changed history when she refused to ride in the back of the bus. Ringgold mixes fantasy and fact in a lovely book that not only tells the Rosa Parks story, but paints a picture of segregation and those who led the Civil Rights movement. 5–9.

Talk About It!

Language

Suppose you could interview Rosa Parks. What questions would you want to ask her? Do you think you would have the courage to do what she did? Do you think that one person alone can change history?

Write It!

Tale of Talking Teeth **Writing**

If you could bring an inanimate object to life, what would it be? The notion of an inanimate object being able to talk and tell about things in the past can be used to inspire young writers to research other events in history. What objects would you use to tell the story of Columbus? For example:

- What if the Niña, the Pinta, & the Santa Maria could talk?
- Or what could the Mayflower tell about the Pilgrims and their crossing?
- What if George Washington's false teeth could talk?

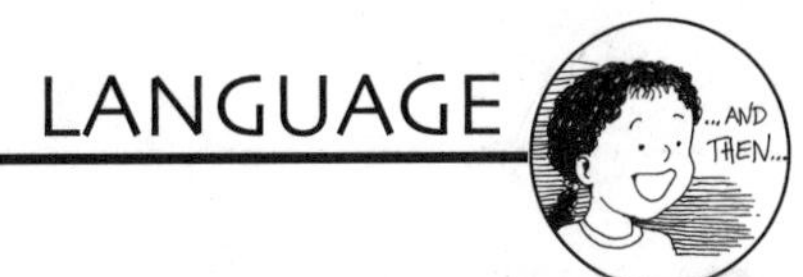

• What would the Apollo spaceship say about its historic voyage? Or the lunar rover?

Play It!

Rod Puppets — Art

Instead of writing what the Mayflower might have said if it could speak, tell it with special rod puppets.

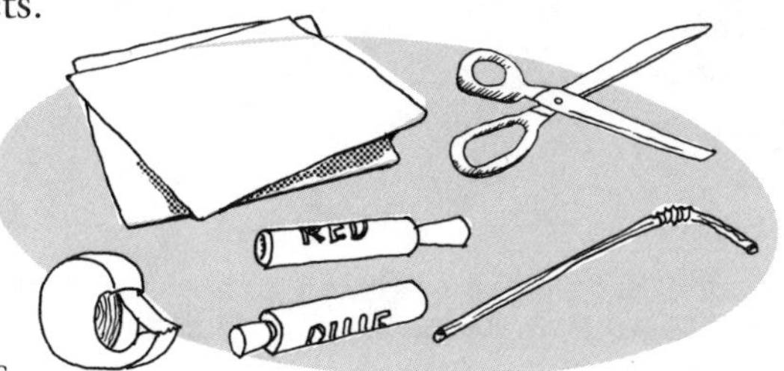

You'll need:

- posterboard
- scissors
- tape
- markers
- flexible drinking straws

Step 1. Draw the inanimate object(s) and cut them out.

Step 2. Tape drinking straw to the back of the picture that you will use to move your puppet.

Step 3. Now, on with the show! Let's hear about how the Atlantic looked from the mast, or the earth from outer space.

WHAT THEY LEARN. Blending fact with fiction gives kids greater freedom to use what they know in imaginative ways.

Read It!

I Will Never Not Ever Eat a Tomato

(by Lauren Child, Candlewick) If you know a finicky eater like Lola, you might want to take a lesson from her big sister Charlie! Lola has a mile-long list of foods she will never eat. But fear not—Charlie dubs carrots "orange twiglets" and mashed potatoes "cloud fluff." Now what would you rename a tomato? 4–8.

Play It!

Vegetable Salad Game | **Active Play**

- This is a group game for 6–9s. Players sit in a circle of chairs.
- Tell children you are going to give them each a veggie name. When you call that name, they must quickly switch seats with other veggies by the same name.

- Go around the circle and touch each child as you say peas, carrots, or tomatoes. Now ask the peas to stand; next the carrots; next the tomatoes.
- Okay, now you are almost ready to play. Just one thing more: take away one chair. Player without a chair will be "It."
- When you call "Peas," "It" and all the Peas must rush for a chair. "It"

keeps changing, so no one remains in the circle for long.

WHAT THEY LEARN. Kids need to remember their new names and listen for them to be called. 6s & up love this active listening game.

Paste it! Taste it! Art

You'll need:

- a supply of magazines
- fabric scraps
- scissors, markers, glue

Look again at the artwork in *I Will Never Not Ever Eat a Tomato.* Instead of simply painting or drawing all the pictures, the illustrator has made collages using pieces of fabric, and photos of veggies, bowls, and dishes all mixed in with her drawings. Encourage kids to make a collage collection of some of their favorite (or least favorite) foods and give them new names. Make a big poster or a book with a page for each food and its new name.

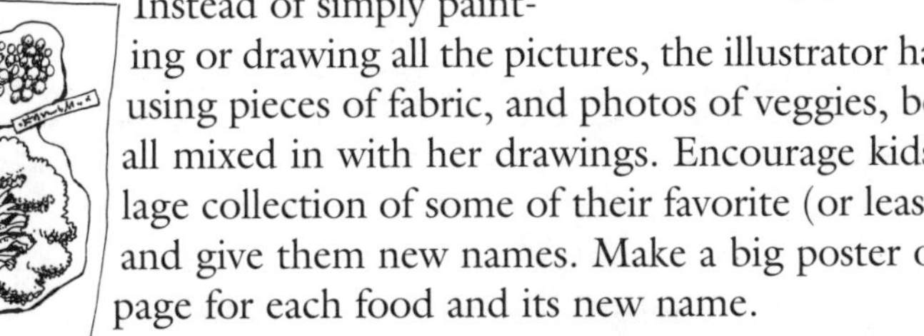

Make A Menu Language

What's for dinner? Brainstorm with your child and write down new and catchy names, à la Charlie, for each of the foods you are going to serve. Kids will like announcing the new names and helping to serve the meal.

WHAT THEY LEARN. Coming up with selling names might help a finicky eater, as it did Lola. But even if it doesn't improve eating habits, the games here involve word play with a touch of humor.

Read It!

Joseph Had a Little Overcoat
(by Simms Taback, Viking) When Joseph's coat gets worn out he turns it into a jacket, and when that wears out, he turns it into a vest. Again and again, Joseph transforms what's left of his coat into a new piece of clothing, until he has nothing but the makings of a book that is a visual delight! 3–7.

Play It!

Dressing for Success — Pretend Play

Kids love to play dress up, and lots of good dress-up clothes are in your closet or drawers. Using real clothes and accessories often has more appeal than store-bought kiddie costumes. Here are some very desirable items to put in the dress-up box that kids can dip into for pretend play:

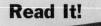

Pocketbooks	Hats	Scarves	Jackets	Shoes
Briefcase	Jewelry	Skirts	Vest	Gloves

Handmade Head Gear — Pretend Play

Preschoolers don't need all the pieces. Their active imagination and one small prop are often all they need to step into role play. A wand, a crown, a cape, a homemade badge can transform little pretenders into a magician, a queen, or a superhero. Roles often come to life with nothing more than an easily made "hat" that helps with the transformation:

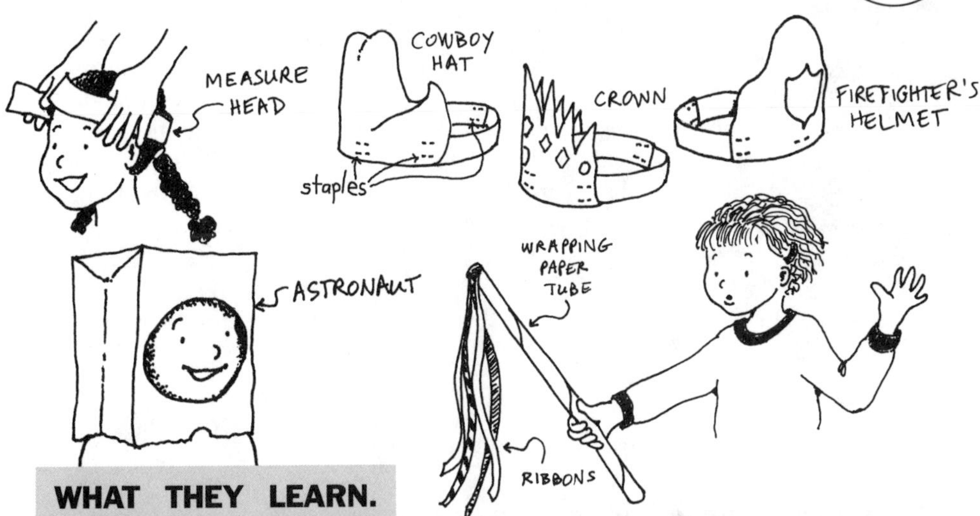

WHAT THEY LEARN. Costumes allow kids to pretend with their whole beings—giving them the freedom to use their full range of voices and body movements to bring their characters to life. Whether it's with a costume or passing an imaginary glass of water, these are ways to nurture their imagination.

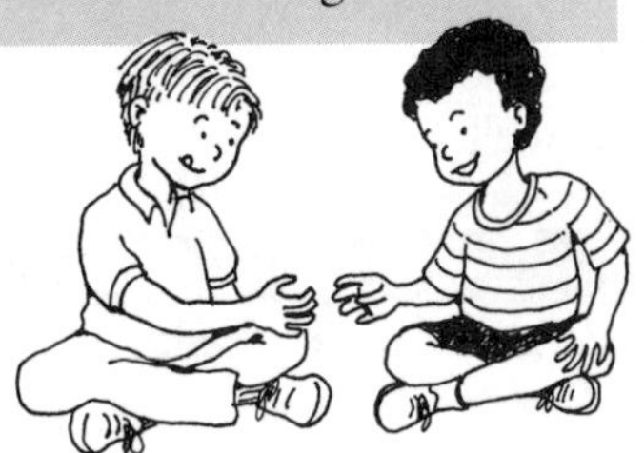

Pass the Water, Please!

Joseph made something from nothing. Now it's your turn to do something with nothing. Pretend you have a full glass of water that you need to give to your friend. Be careful! Don't spill it! Pass it very carefully from one person to the next. If you get it back before someone comes up with the idea of drinking it, pretend to drink it up and then start passing a hot muffin or a beautiful smelling flower. How about something that is very heavy? Keep changing the imagined object and involve kids in acting without speaking. This is an active but quiet game for the family or a small group.

Read It!

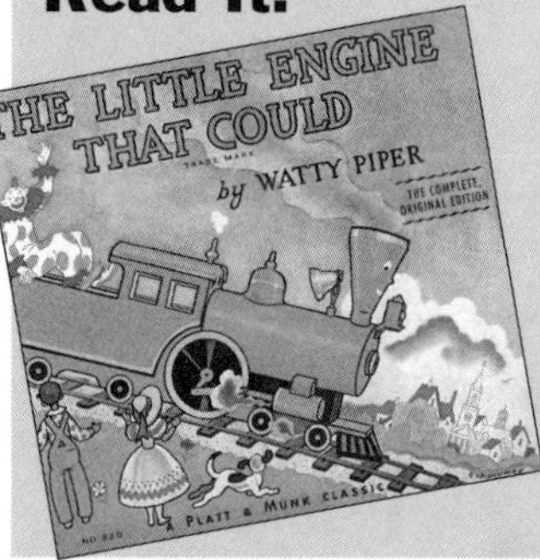

The Little Engine That Could

(by Watty Piper, Penguin) What child has not heard the story of the Little Blue Engine who thought that others would help him get over the mountain with milk and toys for the little children? When others are unable or unwilling to help, it's the Little Engine who finds the strength to do the seemingly impossible! That chant, "I think I can, I think I can," is not lost on small children who are eager for independence yet often fearful of it, too. 3–5.

Play It!

Both girls and boys relate to the struggles and happy ending of this classic story. They enjoy replaying it with their toy trains and props, chanting "I think I can!" Replaying the story calls for recalling the order in which the haughty new engine and the rusty old engine appear. If the mood is right, you might take some of these parts or the parts of the toy clown or little doll who plead for help. Go ahead and ham it up! Playing pretend with miniature props is another important way that children learn about telling stories, those they have heard and their own, as well.

WHAT THEY LEARN. Role playing calls for retelling a story in their own words and recalling the sequence of events needed to make a beginning, middle, and end.

Choo-Choo Cake — Kitchen Science

For the train buff, a cake shaped like a train is easy and fun to make with several cars baked in small individual loaf pans and decorated on a long board with cookie wheels and candy and icing trims that kids can put on.

As they mix the batter, count with them how many stirs they need to get all the lumps out. Talk about what happens to the dry ingredients as they mix them with egg and other liquids. How does the powdery flour look after 10 stirs? 30? How many to make a smooth batter?

How long a cake are you going to make? Have older siblings figure out how many packages of mix you'll need (or how many batches of batter from a recipe). If each package of mix makes three train cars in little loaf pans, how many packages will you need to make a train 10 cars long?

WHAT THEY LEARN. A little science, a bit of math and delight in making something real!

Musical Stop-and Go-Train Game — Active Play

Have children line up like a train, putting hands on the shoulders of child directly in front of them. Tell them that they are the train and they should move when the music plays. But the train must stop when the music stops. This is a cooperative game rather than competitive. **Variation:** If you are using a piano or drum for the music, play it fast and slow, so that train must follow the tempo of the music.

WHAT THEY LEARN. Both of these games develop your child's ability to process auditory information, and are enjoyed by preschoolers and early-school-age kids.

Read It!

Olivia Saves the Circus

(by Ian Falconer, Atheneum) What did Olivia do during her school vacation? Leave it to Olivia to go hog wild with an imaginative account of an unbelievable trip to the circus, starring you know who! Her tale could curl a pig's tail! Olivia is the star of stars! It's a three-ring show with Olivia in every ring! Move over Miss Piggy, Olivia is a swine divine! 4–8.

Play It!

Storytelling á la Olivia! — Language

Making up a tall tale like Olivia's involves creative thinking. Suppose you and your child had to tell what you did over the weekend. Maybe you went shopping or to Grandma's. How about spinning a big fantasy adventure á la Olivia? To get your young storytellers started, tell a tall tale together. Take turns with all the players, encouraging them to add something ridiculous as the story grows. Suppose you were Olivia and you went fishing. What would you probably catch first? next? last? Each player adds something, but must also repeat all the other things caught! This is a good game for long drives or waiting rooms, and developing memory. Some kids might enjoy drawing pictures with highlights of their adventure.

Circus Time — Active Play

What's the next best thing to going to the circus? Pretending to be in the circus, just like Olivia! Applying make-up is optional. Start the fun with a supply of paper dishes or paper bowls as perfect props for the show.

Balancing Act: How many paper dishes can he stack on his head before they fall?

Tightrope Act: Put tape or string on floor. Put a paper plate on the tightrope walker's head and one on each hand.) Now walk across the rope or taped line without dropping anything.

Juggling Act: Start with one paper plate and toss'n'catch. Add another plate. Can your juggler keep two going? How about three? How about you? Try it!

Kids will dream up other acts such as tumbling, or clown acts with funny faces. Add costumes or face paint, popcorn if the idea really grows.

WHAT THEY LEARN. Keeping a story moving calls for mental agility, while the balancing game takes physical agility. Children benefit from the challenge of both. These kinds of entertaining games give children a sense of can-do. They exercise both mind and body along with the pleasures of shared laughter.

Read It!

The Snowman

(by Raymond Briggs, Random House) In reading this classic wordless book with your child, give him plenty of opportunities to do the telling. Take your time relishing each frame of the story as it unfolds. The fact that there are no words will liberate your child to tell the story in his own words, to read into the pictures for feelings as well as simply taking the story forward. 5–8.

Play It!

The Snowman Comes Back Language

After sharing this story, some children are sad about the snowman melting away. Retelling the story is a good way to bring the Snowman back! Suppose after another snowstorm, the boy makes a new snowman—or how about a snow lady? Where might their adventures take them? Will they fly again, and if so, where? Encourage your child to draw his own story. Art often comes before the telling. Have him dictate his story as you write it down. Or make simple sock puppets to dramatize his own Snowman story.

WHAT THEY LEARN. Wordless picture books let kids tell a story in their own words. The images carry the plot line, but no two children will tell the story the same way. Encouraging them to create further adventures with the same cast of characters adds room for even greater creativity.

Coiled Snowflakes — Art

In Scandinavia, stars, snowflakes, and other ornaments are traditionally made with curls of straw and wood shavings. Most of us don't have straw or wood shavings handy, but these delicate ornaments can be made with narrow strips of white typing paper that are coiled and glued.

You'll need:

- white paper, cut into strips ¼" wide, 5" long
- white glue
- pencil
- hole punch
- ribbon

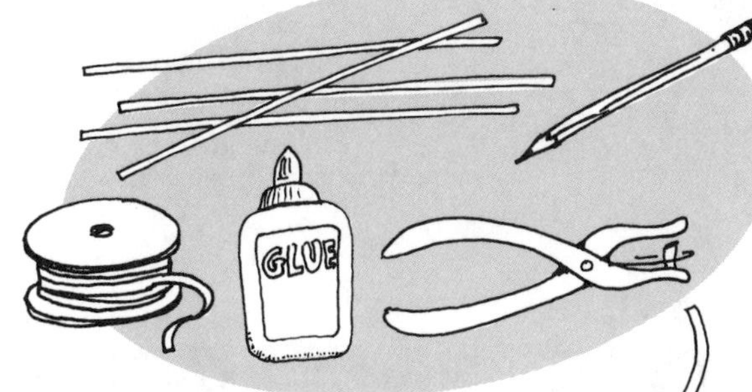

Step 1. Turn strips of paper on pencil, and glue small and large coils. Some of the larger coils can be pressed into long, pointed shapes.

glue end

glue end

coil, glue end, then pinch coil

Step 2. Begin with a coil in the center, and glue a circle of coils around that to form a floral shape.

Step 3. Now begin to alternate long, round, and long coils.

Step 4. Keep a pattern growing until you have a coiled ornament.

Step 5. Hang with a ribbon.

Read It!

So You Want to Be President?

(by Judith St. George/illus. by David Small, Philomel) Maybe you'd like not having to take out the garbage, or having your own personal swimming pool, bowling alley, and movie theatre. But the president has a lot of homework and can't go anywhere alone, and people do not always agree with him! Using funny stories and witty illustrations, this lively, award-winning book introduces young readers to lesser-known presidents with somewhat irreverent snapshots about their habits and families. This is refreshingly unlike the kinds of entries usually found in an encyclopedia. 7 & up.

Write It!

Hail to the Chief — Language

Have kids interview parents, grandparents, and neighbors to find out who was president when they were born. How many presidents have there been since your mom or dad were alive? Who are they? What about your grandparents? How about you? Who was president when you were born? How many people have been president during your life?

Play It!

Heads & Tails Trivia Quiz

What presidents are pictured on the coins and bills we use? How many can you name without looking? Were you right?

Ay, There's the Rub! Art

Try making money with a pencil and paper. It's simple. Put a coin under a sheet of plain paper and rub your pencil over the coin. Abracadabra! A president will appear!

Profile Portraits of Young Americans Science

Using a bright light from a bare bulb lamp, trace your child's shadow profile onto a large sheet of dark paper. Cut it out and mount it on lighter paper. Trace and cut a duplicate for the Portrait Cake (below). Encourage your child to think about how she will help people when she becomes president.

Bake It!

Portrait Cake Kitchen Science

Use any cake mix of your choice to make a large oblong single-layer sheet cake. Allow it to cool, and frost with chocolate frosting. Now put one of your child's Profile Portraits (from above) on the icing. Use confectioner's sugar to dust the cake. Carefully remove the portrait and, voilà! you have a Future President's Portrait Cake!

Read It!

The True Story of the 3 Little Pigs!
(by Jon Scieszka/illus. by Lane Smith, Viking) At last, thanks to a fellow by the name of A. Wolf, we are privy to what really happened when a poor wolf just wanted to borrow a cup of sugar from a certain pig. Was it his fault that he had a terrible cold, causing him to huff and puff and frighten those nervous-nelly pigs? This is good fun for older kids who are ready to begin thinking about how a character's point of view can change a story. 6–9.

Play It!

Make-a-Movie — **Language, Art**

Kids like to tell stories with drawings that unwind to illustrate their tale. Have your child illustrate a story they know well (such as "The Three Pigs"), or a story sequel to a familiar tale, taking the point of view of a different character. This kind of "film-making" also works well for making "TV" shows and commercials or illustrating a song.

You'll need:

- a roll of plain shelving paper
- markers & crayons
- a cardboard box about the same height as paper roll
- wooden dowels or cardboard rollers from gift wrap

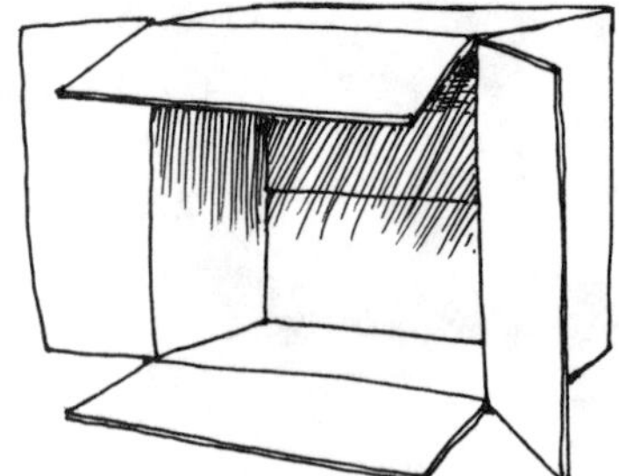

Step 1. A roll of white shelving paper and a batch of markers are all they need to draw a "movie" that can be unrolled to give a show.

Step 2. (Adult help will be needed to make the screening box for the "film.") Cut flaps off of one side of box to make the "screen." Cut two holes in top and two below where wooden dowels will fit.

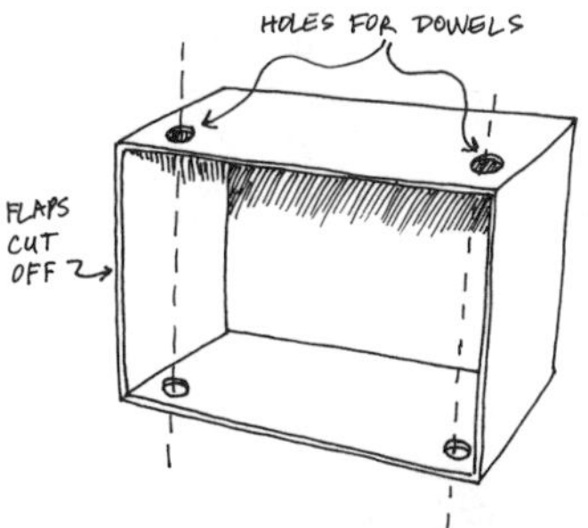

Step 3. Tape the "movie" to the dowels and kids can roll their film as they narrate a story or sing a song that they have illustrated.

WHAT THEY LEARN. Sequencing a story or a song visually is a challenge to children's memory as well as their comprehension. Somehow the extra-long piece of paper sparks inventive and expansive drawings. Next, they'll love hamming it up by putting on a show—all they need is an audience—you!

Commercial Tie-Ins

Dream up some good ads as sponsors for the show. How about a Big Bad Wolf Toothpaste, or Curlers for Pig-tails? Drawing the art and making up the jingles or ad copy to narrate them can be amusing to both the artist and the listener.

Read It!

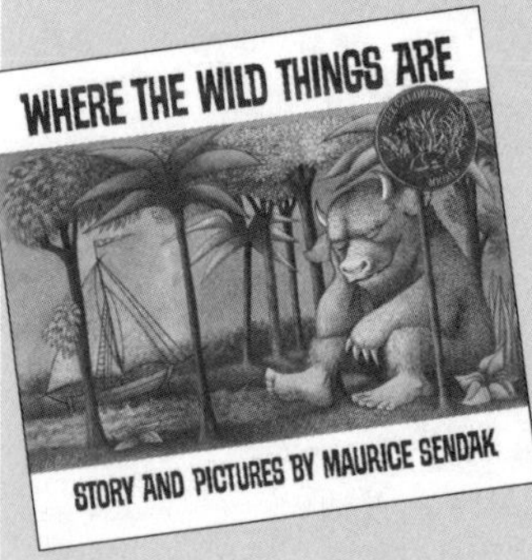

Where the Wild Things Are
(by Maurice Sendak, HarperCollins) Old preschoolers and young school-aged kids have long loved the mischievous Max who gets punished by being sent to his room without dinner. Max takes off to the land of the Wild Things, on one of the most remarkable fantasy romps in children's literature. Some fours may enjoy this, but it's a better choice for slightly older kids who understand the difference between real and make-believe. 5–8.

Play It!

Oh, You Wild Thing! — Art

Children are usually enthralled by the look of those humanoid creatures that romp with Max. With a lump of clay kids can make their very own Wild Thing. Before they begin, look together at the features of the Wild Things: their big feet, noses, ears, and horns. (The object is not to have them trying to copy Sendak's art, but rather to find inspiration in the art and create their own.) After they are finished sculpting, older kids may want to dry and paint their creatures, name them, and even tell their own stories.

...AND THEN...

Make-a-Mask — Art

Use big paper plates with construction paper cut-outs and glue to design far-out Wild Things mask that can be displayed or used. Be sure to make eye openings big enough for safe and easy viewing. What about making a mask of a Wild Thing's Pet? What kind of pet would a Wild Thing have? Play a bit of spooky music such as "Danse Macabre" by Saint-Saens and turn the lights low as your Wild Things shake-a-leg with their masks.

Make-an-Ad — Language

Draw a billboard picture of your own Wild Thing and have it sell some remedy. For example:

> My Wild Thing says,
> "Drink **Wild Thing Punch**!
> It's a Knockout of a Drink!"

or

> My Wild Thing Swears By
> **Running Wild Sneakers**
> —Speedy as Lightning!

Brainstorm other products Wild Things might endorse, and develop an ad campaign!

WHAT THEY LEARN. Playing around with monsters often gives kids a sense of control over things they may fear. Making up ads also lets them begin to understand how products get sold.

My Wild Thing Says
DRink Wild
Thing Punch
Pun

Read It!

Look-Alikes Jr.

(by Joan Steiner, Little Brown) A sequel to the original award winner, *Look-Alikes,* this visual feast inspires young "readers" to look at the surprising details that make up the mini-world settings Steiner has composed and photographed with pretzels, crayons, and other familiar objects. These are the type of pages that kids (and adults) love to pore over—always seeing something new. 4–8.

Play It!

Crunchy Cookie Castle — Art

Make a cookie or cracker house with your child for a party. Take your inspiration from Steiner's book, but keep everything you assemble "good enough to eat" so it won't be wasted. Use a clean box covered with foil to make the "infra-structure."

Joanne's Confectioner's Sugar Glue

½ cup confectioner's sugar
1–2 tsp. water

Stir water into the confectioner's sugar until the sugar becomes a smooth paste. It should be spreadable and white like icing. If it is runny, add sugar; if it's too dry, add a bit more water.

Use candies with flat bottom surfaces for trims—gum drops, kisses, M&Ms, etc.

Variation: Cracker Box Cottage

Use crackers and try peanut butter as glue. Use thin pretzel sticks for trims, corn chips for a textured roof, and your imagination. Kids love serving a treat they've made at a holiday gathering!

Doll House — Art

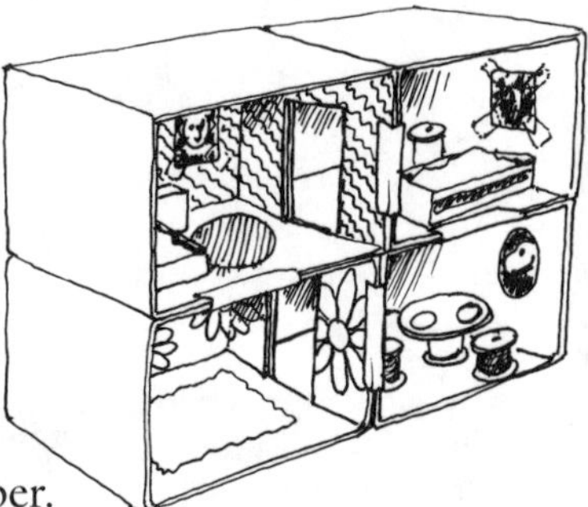

Make a doll house and furnish it with materials found in your home. To make a two-or-more-storey house, use several shoe boxes taped together. An adult will need to tape the boxes together and cut doorways, but kids will enjoy painting the interiors or pasting gift wrap as wall paper. Now, how about furniture? School-aged kids have the dexterity to make miniatures with found materials, e.g., thread spools make tables, small boxes make beds, etc. Kids will also enjoy hearing the story of *The Littles* or *The Borrowers.*

WHAT THEY LEARN. Looking at details in the book not only sharpens their visual perception, it can inspire creative thinking. Making constructions of their own gives them a chance to try some of that "outside-the-box" thinking.

Make a "Sounds Alike" Book — Language

How many words can you and your child think of that may sound alike but mean different things (otherwise known as homophones)? Put them in a book for your child to illustrate—words such as nose/knows, flower/flour, two/to, red/read, dear/deer, shoe/shoo, write/right...

Read It!

Look Book

(by Tana Hoban, Greenwillow) Do you know what a butterfly looks like? What if you could only see a patch of butterfly? Tana Hoban covers all but a small detail of a photo and the reader must guess what is hidden below. Turn the black cut-out page to see the whole object. In this collection she shows the object as a detail, in a full photo, and then again, in context with the bigger scene. These are good talking books that encourage children to look more closely at details. 4–8.

Play It!

Look Some More — Art

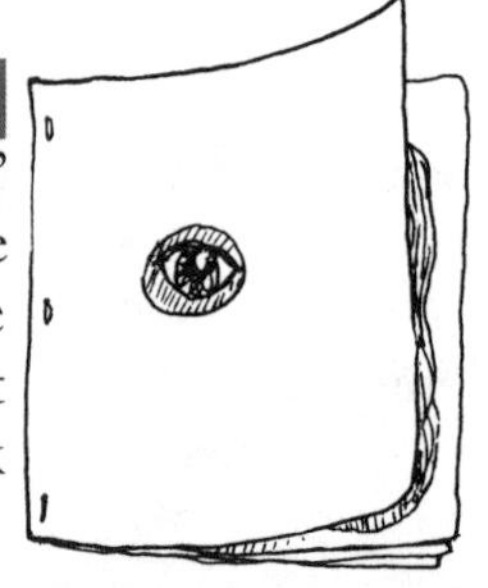

Children will enjoy making their own "Look Books." Start with photos they can cut out of magazines. Choose a detail in that photo and cut out a "window" in a piece of construction paper that allows them to cover all but the detail. Put a collection together into a Look Book that they can share with a friend.

Snap Shooter Book — Art

Give your child a disposable camera and challenge him to take pictures of familiar objects with interesting details. For example, the bark of a tree, your dog or cat, siding on a building, wooden flooring, a piece of fabric with interesting texture. Their objective will be

to zoom in close enough to capture the detail but still show the whole object. Choose the best of these and put them in a small photo album with see-through pages. In every other page, put construction paper with cut-out windows that frame a detail and turn to reveal the full photo on the next page.

Find a Shape — Math

Tana Hoban likes to look for details such as shapes as well as textures. When you have spare time, turn it into a looking adventure. How many objects in the room or in a photo can you find that are round? square? rectangular? triangular? A fun game that requires nothing more than using your eyes to find a surprise.

WHAT THEY LEARN. Many children are "global" lookers—they get a quick view of things and look no further. Yet learning to look at details is a skill that is needed not only to appreciate beauty. Whether they are reading a story, doing a math problem, working on a science experiment—details make all the difference. This is an entertaining way to introduce that more detailed way of looking.

Read It!

Max

(by Bob Graham, Candlewick) Despite the fact that his superhero parents and grandparents can fly, young Max can't seem to get off the ground! But one day, stirred by the needs of another, Max puts someone else's fears before his own. A reassuring tale for kids who often worry about living up to expectations—their own as well as others'. 5–8.

Play It!

Fingerprint Art

Among the things that make you uniquely you are your fingerprints. Though they may look similar, no two people have exactly the same prints. You can explain this to your child, but showing her is even better. Use your fingerprints to make some original art, too.

You'll need:

- washable inkpad
- paper
- skinny markers

Step 1. Press index finger tip on ink pad and then carefully roll the fingertip on clean paper.

Step 2. Add face features, legs, arms, hats, and other details to turn your finger prints into mini creatures. These are scaled perfectly for thank-you notes, greeting cards, or cartoons. They don't need any practical purpose—they are fun to make for their own sake. For more inspiration, see *Ed Emberley's Fingerprint Drawing Book*.

WHAT THEY LEARN. School-aged kids sometimes get critical or self conscious about their ability to make realistic pictures. Giving them "cartooning" techniques that allow for non-realistic images frees them to make playful representations. These playful figures also call for the fine motor skills needed for writing.

Write It! **Language**

Now that Max can fly, what new adventures will he find? Where will he go with his newfound ability to soar? Your child might like to draw the story and then dictate or write it. Often the story comes more easily after the art.

Read It!

Max Found Two Sticks

(by Brian Pinkney, Simon & Schuster) Inventive Max's first drumsticks come from a city tree. He "drums" on his legs, on garbage cans and whatever else that will resonate. For a grand finale, a real band comes down the street and one of the players tosses Max real drumsticks! If your child has ever turned a pot into a drum, or dreamed of being in a parade and making music, this is likely to inspire more creative drumming. 4–8.

Play It!

Tape-A-Drum — Art

From the time they are old enough to bang a spoon on the top of a table or hit the bottom of a pot, children delight in drumming. In the beginning it's the power to make something happen. But before long children find pleasure in varying the speed and sound of the beat. Before long they can repeat a beat or follow the beat of music. All of these playful activities play a role in developing their auditory discrimination—skills they will need for academic as well as social interactions. It's easy to make a drum with rich sounds.

You'll need:

- large empty cans from coffee, tomatoes, or juice
- wide transparent packing tape
- permanent markers (optional)
- dowels for drum sticks
- construction paper (optional)

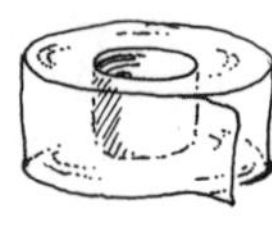

Step 1. Remove top and bottom of can. You'll need to smooth the inside of the can so that there are no small sharp edges inside.

Step 2. Child can decorate can with permanent markers, or use with or without labels. You can also cover cans with construction paper.

Step 3. To make a tall bongo-style drum, tape two or more cans together in a tower. The more cans you stack, the deeper the sound you will get.

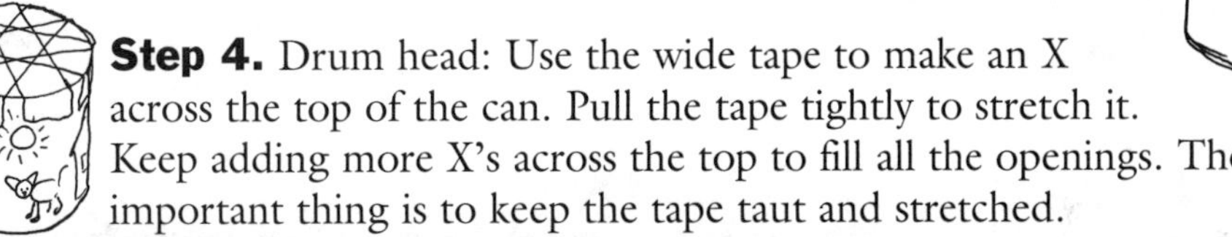

Step 4. Drum head: Use the wide tape to make an X across the top of the can. Pull the tape tightly to stretch it. Keep adding more X's across the top to fill all the openings. The important thing is to keep the tape taut and stretched.

Drumming Games — Language

Echo Play

Play a simple rhythmic pattern such as "fast—slow—fast—slow." Ask child to repeat it. If the pattern is too hard, make it simpler. Play this game with a variety of patterns that become increasingly complex.

Name My Tune

Without singing or using words, use your drum to tap out the rhythm of a familiar song such as "Jingle Bells" or "Row, Row, Row Your Boat." Can your child name that tune? Try several familiar tunes and switch roles with other players, being a listener as well as a player.

WHAT THEY LEARN. Playful way to build auditory memory.

Read It!

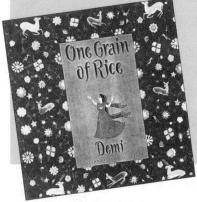

One Grain of Rice

(by Demi, Scholastic) A selfish raja does not share the rice his people grow. Rani, a clever girl, returns some spilled rice and the raja grants her a wish. She asks only for one grain of rice, but she wants it doubled every day for thirty days. The raja agrees, not understanding how such a seemingly small request can grow into more than a billion grains! 7 & up.

Play It!

Rice Painting — Art

How do you paint with rice? It's easy.

You'll need:
- heavy paper or cardboard
- white glue • colored rice

You say your rice is all white? Relax—you can color your rice with a splash of water and some food coloring.

Step 1. Put a half cup of rice in a jar and add an eighth of a cup of water and a splash of food coloring.

Step 2. Shake the rice until it is completely coated. Pour the rice on a paper towel that is spread on a cookie sheet. Allow it to dry. This should take about a half an hour. Now stir up a few more batches of rice in different colors. Store various colors in separate containers.

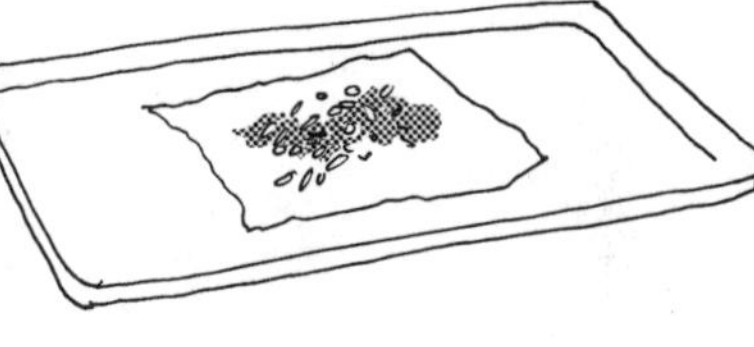

Step 3. Draw a design or scene with a pencil. Spread glue to cover an area that should be a single color.

Step 4. Sprinkle the single color of rice on that area and allow it to dry. Shake the loose rice back into its container. Now spread glue over another area that is to be a second color.

Step 5. Continue until the composition is complete.

WHAT THEY LEARN.
Coloring the rice and learning the technique of gluing one area at a time calls for patience and working in an orderly sequential way—important work habits that school-aged kids need to learn.

Read It!

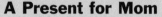

A Present for Mom

(by Vivian French/illus. by Dana Kubick, Candlewick) Stanley, the youngest kitten in the family, is having trouble finding the right gift for Mother's Day. His big sisters and brother each have the perfect gift. But after a great deal of worry, clever little Stanley comes up with a gift box that Mom loves! Totally priceless and charming! 3–6.

Play It!

Hand Prints — Art

Use self-hardening clay to produce keepsakes that you and Grandma and Grandpa will love to have.

You'll need:

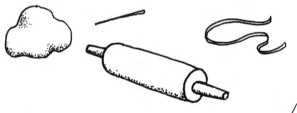

- clay
- toothpick
- rolling pin
- ribbon

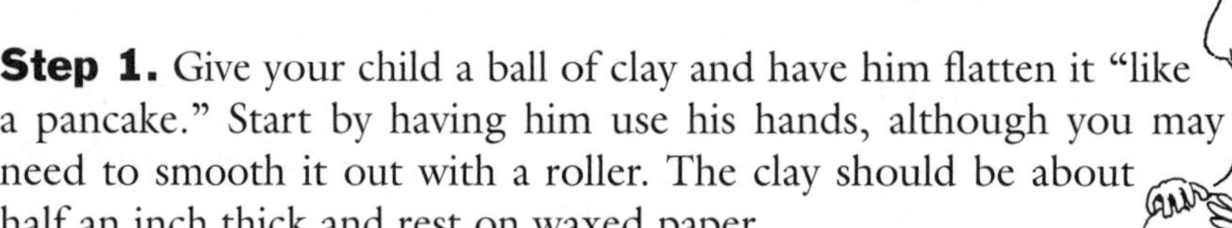

Step 1. Give your child a ball of clay and have him flatten it "like a pancake." Start by having him use his hands, although you may need to smooth it out with a roller. The clay should be about half an inch thick and rest on waxed paper.

Step 2. Now have your child put one hand on the clay and hold his fingers very still. Use a dull butter knife to trace around his fingers until you have a clean outline of his hand.

Step 3. Carefully pull the excess clay away from the handprint and cut a straight edge off above the wrist.

Step 4. With a toothpick, make a small hole in the top that you can thread with a ribbon for hanging. Use the toothpick to print your child's name and the date somewhere on the hand.

Step 5. Allow the clay hand to dry completely. This may take a few days, depending on the humidity. Your child can paint the hand with acrylic paint that you can cover with a glaze for a shine.

WHAT THEY LEARN. In time your child will see how much he has grown, but for now, just seeing how the soft clay hardens is fascinating. Give him plenty of opportunities to experiment with clay and other materials that he can shape in his two hands. He'll like experimenting with tracing his hand on paper, too.

Read It!

Seven Spools of Thread

(by Angela S. Medearis/illus. by Daniel Minter, Albert Whitman) In a village in Ghana, seven brothers quarrel from day to night. When their father dies, his will says that he leaves his possessions to them only if they can turn the seven spools of colored thread into gold by sundown. Although this is called a Kwanzaa story, it is a timeless tale about working together for a common good. 5 & up.

Play It!

Paper Weaving — Art

Celebrate Kwanzaa by weaving special placemats with construction paper in Kente colors.

You'll need:

- construction paper in black, orange, red, yellow
- scissors

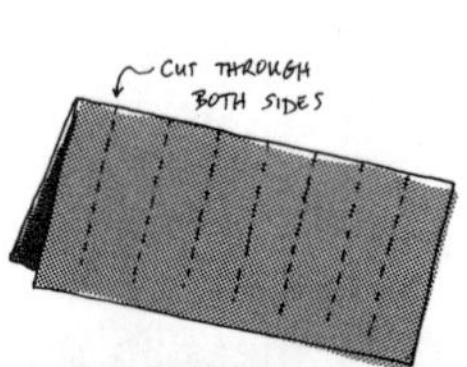

Step 1. Fold the black paper in half the long way.

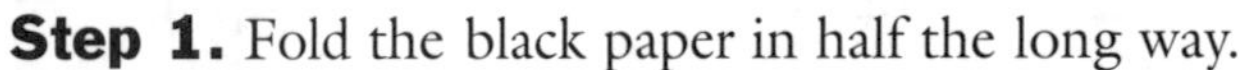

Step 2. Cut the paper, starting on the crease as shown at right: Unfold the paper again.

Step 3. Cut one-inch-wide strips of the other colored construction paper. Each strip should be as long as the black paper.

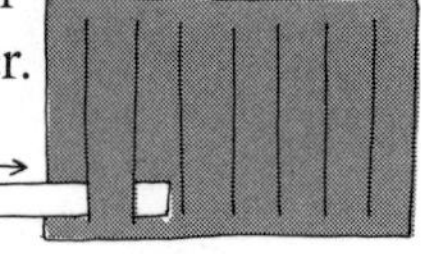

Step 4. Weave one colored strip over and under through the black paper.

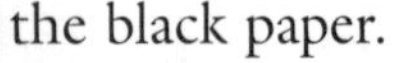

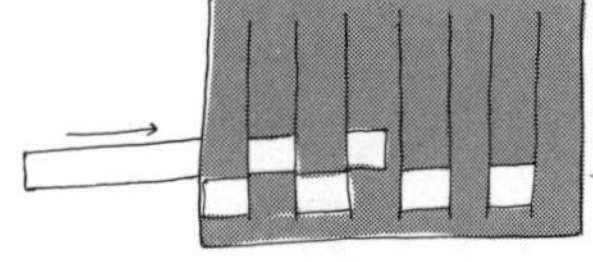

Step 5. Weave a new color directly above the first piece, but start this one under and then over.

Step 6. Continue adding strips, alternating where you start on each line until all the spaces are filled up.

Step 7. Kids can paste down the loose ends, but this is optional. The place mat is now ready to use.

WHAT THEY LEARN. Paper weaving demands dexterity as well as visual perception and paying attention to details of a repeated pattern as they complete a task.

Variation

Cut the black paper with wavy lines, and the weaving will have a different look.

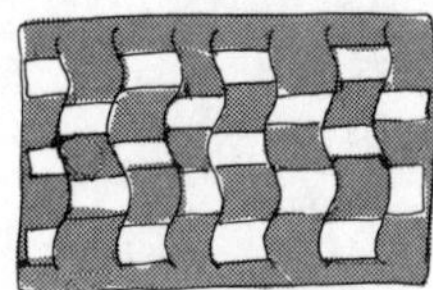

Candlestick Holders — Art

In the season of lights, an extra pair of candlesticks is always welcome! You'll need some self-hardening clay and a candle.

Step 1. Have your child roll two balls of clay, bigger than a golf ball but smaller than a baseball. Press the bottom of the ball flat against a tabletop to make the bottom level.

Step 2. Have her put a textured design on each ball with toothpicks, a fork, fingerprints, or other found objects. (Avoid adding on pieces of clay, as they are likely to fall off when the clay dries.)

Step 3. Press a candle into the center, making a steady place where the candle will fit. Now remove the candle and allow the candlesticks to dry for several days.

Step 4. Once dry, they can be painted with matching designs. These make good gifts for adult family members. Wrap them in tissue paper and bows.

ART

Read It!

Snow

(by Uri Shulevitz, Farrar Straus) First there is no snow, then a single flake and great hope. Though the adults all have doubts, one small boy keeps hope alive. This is a quiet book that captures the look, feel, and wonder of a snowfall. Once they know the story, encourage children to retell it in their own words by using the pictures. 4–8.

Play It!

Snow Globe — Art

Longing for a flurry of snowflakes? It's easy! Make a snow globe.

You'll need:

- small clear plastic jars with screw-on lids (plastic is safer than glass for kids to handle). We found that plastic peanut butter containers work well.

- small plastic toys (small figures, trees, vehicles, animals)

- silver or white glitter
- waterproof epoxy
- water or baby oil
- if using water, a few drops of glycerin (optional; found in drug store)

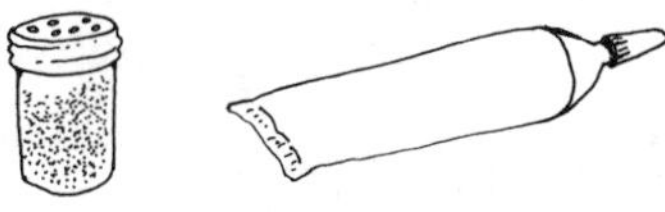

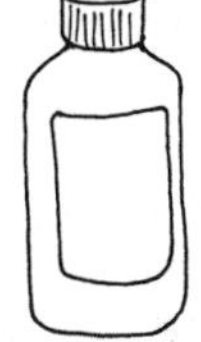

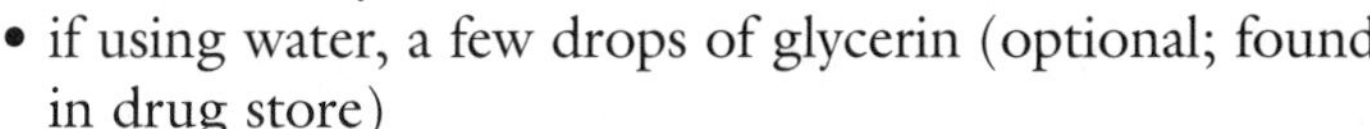

Step 1. Build up a base of floral clay inside the lid. Attach the figures to make a scene in the lid.

Step 2. Fill jar with either baby oil or water; add a half-teaspoon of glitter. If using water, add a splash of glycerin, which will make the glitter fall slowly.

Step 3. Screw the lid on firmly.

Step 4. Seal with waterproof epoxy (must be done by an adult). Apply to inside of lid and screw the lid on firmly. Allow seal to harden for 24 hours.

Step 5. Turn the jar over and let there be snow!

WHAT THEY LEARN. Snow globes are perennial favorites. In making their own, children can choose their own theme and scene. These make great gifts for a parent, grandparent, or teacher's desk.

Read It!

The Story About Ping

(by Marjorie Flack/illus. by Kurt Wiese, Viking) Last one home gets a swat on the tail feathers. Being an adventuresome little duck Ping tries to avoid the consequences. Like Peter Rabbit, Ping discovers that living by the rules with his family may be a lot safer than life on the Yangtze River on his own. Generations of children have enjoyed Ping's harrowing adventure and happy return home! 4–8.

Play It!

Paper Lanterns — Art

In China the Lunar New Year is celebrated for 15 days. A Lantern Festival is held on the last day of festivities as friends and family carry bright-colored paper lanterns and feast together on sticky rice balls. Make your own paper lantern! Make one in a different color for each member of the family.

You'll need:

- colored construction paper
- scissors
- paper punch
- yarn
- stapler or glue

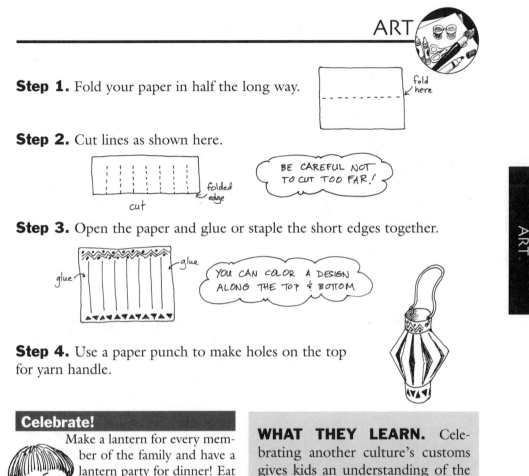

Step 1. Fold your paper in half the long way.

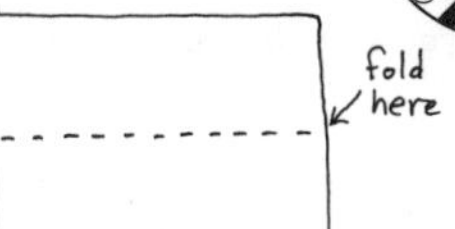

Step 2. Cut lines as shown here.

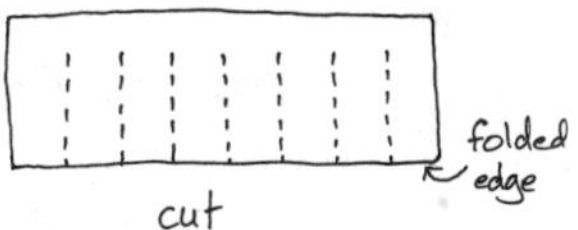

BE CAREFUL NOT
TO CUT TOO FAR!

Step 3. Open the paper and glue or staple the short edges together.

glue
glue
YOU CAN COLOR A DESIGN
ALONG THE TOP & BOTTOM

Step 4. Use a paper punch to make holes on the top for yarn handle.

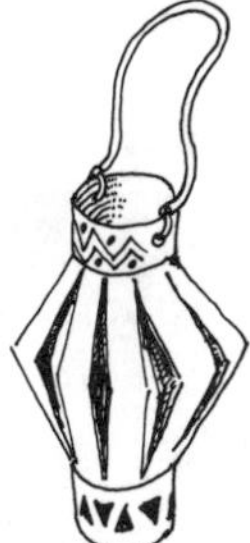

Celebrate!

Make a lantern for every member of the family and have a lantern party for dinner! Eat with chopsticks and try some Chinese food to celebrate your own Lantern Festival! Make placemats (see page 46).

WHAT THEY LEARN. Celebrating another culture's customs gives kids an understanding of the world beyond their doorstep—for young children this is best done by hands-on experiences with different art, food, and music.

Read It!

The Story of Ferdinand

(by Munro Leaf/illus. by Robert Lawson, Viking) As bulls go, Ferdinand is a rugged individualist! He does not want to fight in the bullring or anywhere else, for that matter! Published in 1936, this classic has given heart to generations of children who have grappled with the choice between living up to other people's expectations or being true to oneself. 4–8.

Play It!

Scrunch & Crunch Flowers — Art

Let Ferdinand's love of flowers inspire a garden of floral delights. You may not be able to buy fresh flowers or even pick them, but in no time at all you can make them together. Here's a simple way to create a bouquet of colorful scrunch & crunch flowers—no two flowers will be exactly alike!

You'll need:

- colored tissue paper
- scissors
- pipe cleaners

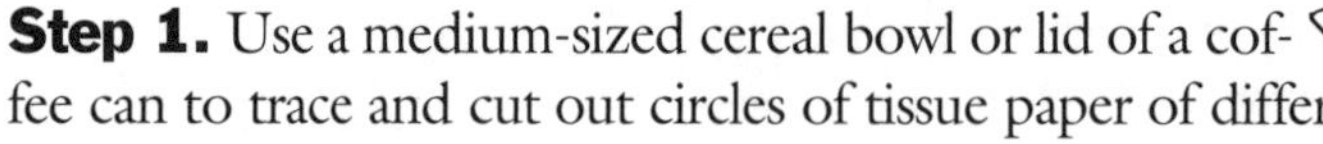

Step 1. Use a medium-sized cereal bowl or lid of a coffee can to trace and cut out circles of tissue paper of differ-

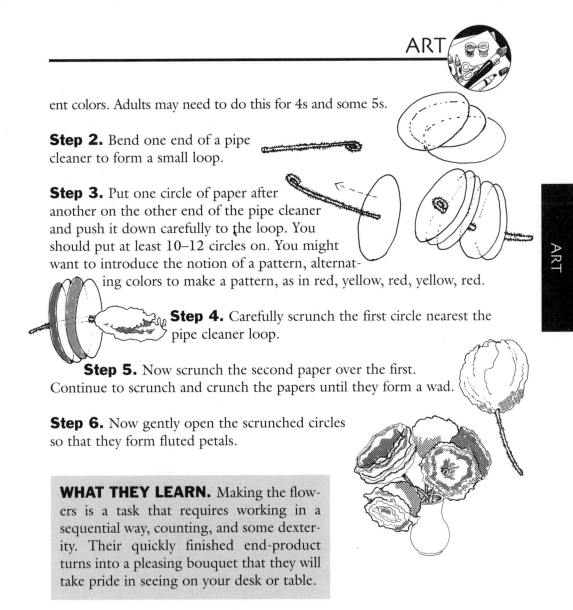

ent colors. Adults may need to do this for 4s and some 5s.

Step 2. Bend one end of a pipe cleaner to form a small loop.

Step 3. Put one circle of paper after another on the other end of the pipe cleaner and push it down carefully to the loop. You should put at least 10–12 circles on. You might want to introduce the notion of a pattern, alternating colors to make a pattern, as in red, yellow, red, yellow, red.

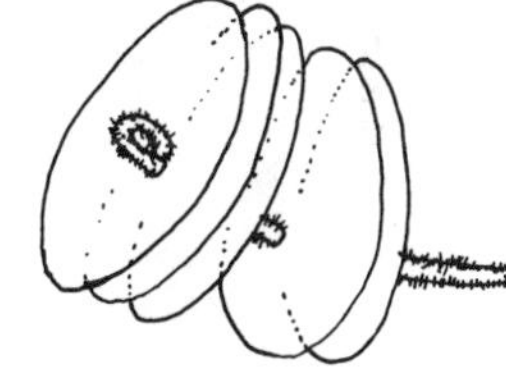

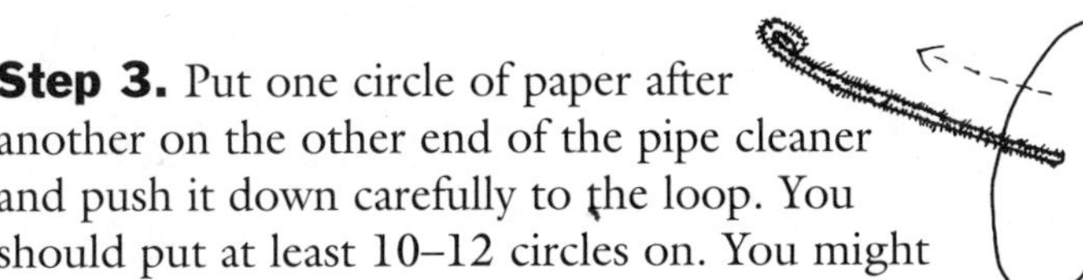

Step 4. Carefully scrunch the first circle nearest the pipe cleaner loop.

Step 5. Now scrunch the second paper over the first. Continue to scrunch and crunch the papers until they form a wad.

Step 6. Now gently open the scrunched circles so that they form fluted petals.

WHAT THEY LEARN. Making the flowers is a task that requires working in a sequential way, counting, and some dexterity. Their quickly finished end-product turns into a pleasing bouquet that they will take pride in seeing on your desk or table.

Read It!

Too Many Tamales

(by Gary Soto/illus. by Ed Martinez, Putnam) It's a mystery! Maria is helping Mama mix the masa for the tamales she is making for the holiday party. Maria just can't resist trying the sparkling ring on her finger and forgets to take it off when she starts kneading the masa again. Where is the ring? How many tamales will Maria and her cousins have to eat to find it? A delicious tale for the holidays! 5–8.

Play It!

Make-a-Piñata — Art

Along with the tamales, what holiday celebration would be complete without a piñata? You don't have to be Latino to enjoy making and breaking a piñata. This is a parent/child project that can't be done in a day, but it's fun to make and use. Here's how you make it:

You'll need:

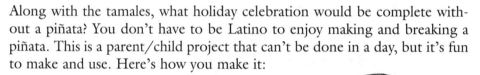

- a good-sized balloon
- string to hang it on
- newspaper torn in inch-wide strips, 4–8" long.
- glue made from flour and water or watered-down Elmer's glue
- tempera paint

Step 1. Blow up the balloon and hang it over the work area. Put plastic or newspapers under the balloon to catch the drips.

Step 2. Get a good supply of paper strips ready.

Step 3. Swirl equal parts of water and flour in a bowl (¼ cup of each). Now an adult needs to add one cup of boiling water to flour mixture. Stir and cool, and you have paste. Or mix equal parts of white glue and water.

Step 4. Dip one strip at a time into the paste. Use your fingers to remove excess paste. Now put it smoothly on the balloon. Continue adding one strip at a time. Overlap strips until the entire balloon is covered. Continue until you have three or four layers of strips on the balloon.

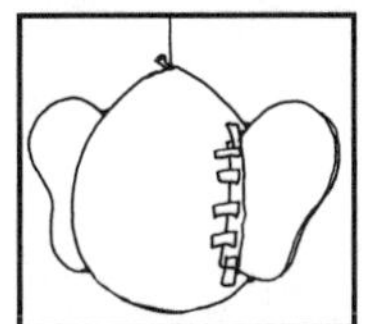

***Note:** If you want to add shaped cones, animal ears, or snouts, you can tape poster board shapes on the balloon before you begin and cover them with paper strips as you build the layers of papier maché.

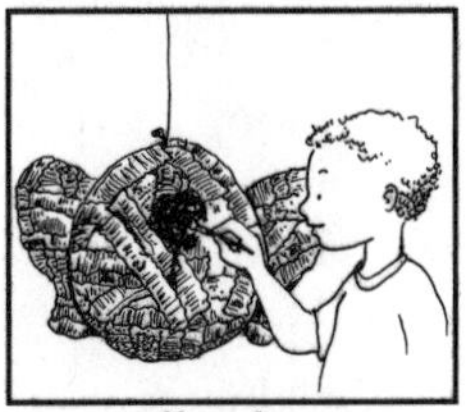

Step 5. Allow the paper to dry for several days.

Step 6. Now it's time to paint the piñata.

Step 7. When the piñata is dry, use a pin to burst the balloon (if it's not already deflated by then). Cut an opening at the top so you can put the candy inside. Make a loop of cord to cradle the pinata and hang it so that kids can use a stick to hit it. Blindfold and spin the players before they try hitting the piñata.

WHAT THEY LEARN. Exploring another culture's traditions can be great fun!

Read It!

When I Was Little

(by Jamie Lee Curtis/illus. by Laura Cornell, HarperCollins) Subtitled *A Four-Year-Old's Memoir of Her Youth*, this spirited narrative contrasts the many ways the young heroine has grown and changed. Both words and pictures capture the "can do" attitude of a little girl who has a very positive sense of how big she has grown. 4–7.

Play It!

Self-Portrait — Art

Life-sized portraits are pleasing to preschoolers, who are always interested in how big they're getting.

You'll need:

- a big piece of brown paper as long as your child
- scissors
- paint, crayons, and markers
- glue
- fabric scraps, ribbons, buttons, patterned gift wrap

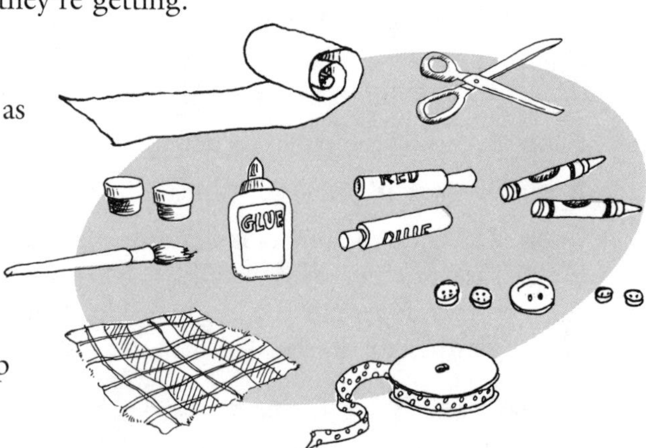

Step 1. Roll out a large piece of brown butcher paper. Put books at all four corners to keep the paper from rolling up.

Step 2. Have your preschooler stretch out as you trace her shape.

Step 3. Now the fun begins. Give your preschooler markers, crayons, scraps of fabric or gift wrap, ribbons, buttons and glue to decorate her self portrait. Dry overnight.

Step 4. Cut out the self-portrait (you do this) and roll up with a ribbon to give as a gift. Use a large mailing tube to send to a grandparent who will enjoy seeing how big the young artist has grown.

WHAT THEY LEARN. Preschoolers are thrilled to have such a large canvas on which to color, collage, and express themselves. The notion of sending something that they made as a gift will also be pleasing to the sender as well as the receiver.

Create-a-Memoir **Language**

Have your child create her own memoir by dictating what she can do now, that she couldn't do when she was little.

..3, 4...

Read It!

Colors Everywhere
(by Tana Hoban, Greenwillow) Each glorious color photo is accompanied by a sidebar with bands of all the colors found in the photo. It's fun to search out the matching bands, to note the details in the photos, and to realize how many colors make up the sights we often take for granted. 3–6.

Play It!

Color Towers — Math

You'll need building bricks, such as Duplos.

To play: Talk about all the colored blocks in the bucket. Make a guess-timate: Are there more red ones? Blue ones? Yellow ones? One way to find out would be to count them. But a more active way would be to make an all-red tower or sideways train. Then make an all-yellow tower. Which is taller?

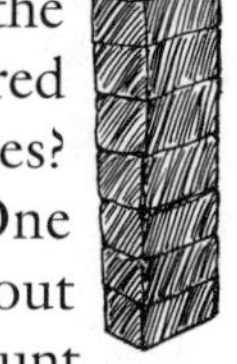

WHAT THEY LEARN. A good game for developing sorting skills, dexterity, and guess-timating more and less.

Play a Pattern — Math

Make a color die that has two blue, two red, and two yellow sides. Now put a basket of blue, red, and yellow Duplo blocks between you. Each player decides what color pattern he'll make. Players take turns tossing the die and

MATH

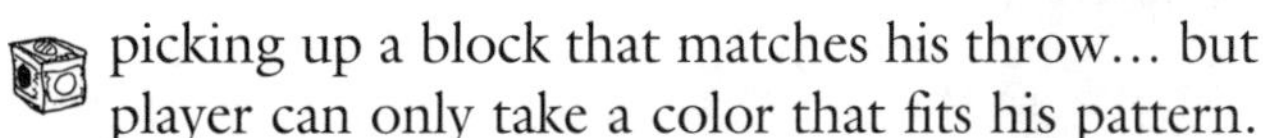

picking up a block that matches his throw… but player can only take a color that fits his pattern. For example: Player 1 may be making a blue, yellow, blue, yellow pattern. Player 2 may be making a blue, yellow, red, blue, yellow, red pattern. Winner is the first player to make a six-piece pattern. For a longer game, make it a ten-piece pattern.

Crayon Muffins — Art

What home doesn't have a collection of old stubby crayons rolling around in drawers? Recycle the old bits and pieces into chunky multi-colored drawing tools. This is a "magical" project, which requires adult participation.

You'll need:

- old yucky crayons
- muffin tin
- paper muffin tin liners

Step 1. Have kids strip the paper off of old crayons. Break the crayons into big pieces. Put several colors in paper cup liners in a muffin tin.

Note: Steps 2 & 3 must be done by an adult.

Step 2. Bake in oven (325°) until the crayons melt (approx. 5–8 min.). Encourage your child to speculate about what will happen to the colors.

Step 3. Remove the tin carefully because the melted wax will be very hot. Allow it to cool completely.

Step 4. When cool, peel the muffin paper to reveal all-new, multi-colored crayon muffin!

WHAT THEY LEARN.
Introduces kids to the idea that solids can be turned into liquids and back to solids again.

Read It!

Gigantic!

(by Patrick O'Brien, Holt) O'Brien compares each of the fourteen prehistoric creatures to modern-day objects with similar features. Although the objects and dinos are not drawn to scale, this is a book that will give kids reason to think about the dinos' amazing sizes and how they compare to things we know. 5–9.

Play It!

Bigger Than a Breadbox? — Math

If you have a "dino-maniac" in your midst, you probably have a good-sized collection of dinosaur figures around, too. It's sometimes hard for kids to imagine or translate the factual material about the size and habits of dinosaurs in concrete ways. *Gigantic!* makes comparisons that make giant sizes come alive. But "measuring" the length of one of these giants in relation to your house or the block you live on will make it all the more understandable.

Step 1. Measure a length of string that is ten feet long. How many tens will it take to equal the length of a 50-foot Gigantosaurus? Use the ten-foot string and a chalk to

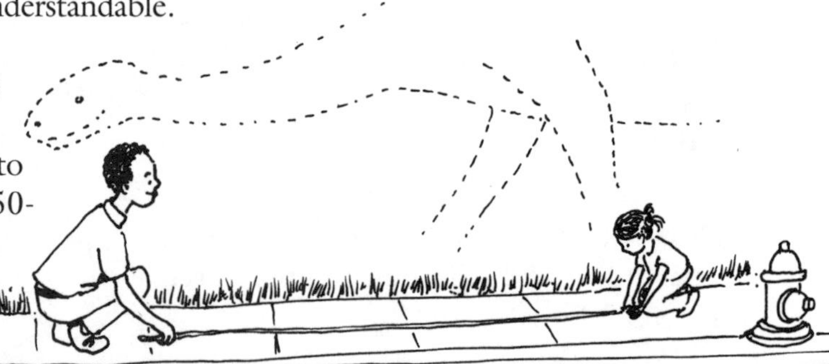

mark where the giant begins and ends on the street where you live.

Step 2. Check out the length and height of some of the other giants.

Step 3. Talk about things they know that are as long or tall as the Gigantosaurus. Was it longer than a bus? longer than your house? longer than the block you live on?

Variations — Math

Have kids count the number of steps they must take to walk 10 feet. Now how many steps must they walk to go 50 feet?

Nobody Ever Saw A Dinosaur — ART

Amazing as this may seem to your child, nobody ever saw a real live breathing dinosaur. So what color were they? Did they have stripes or spots? Kids love to let their imaginations go wild and sculpt dinos with colored non-hardening plasticine or air-dried clay that they can paint when it gets dry. Others prefer to draw their dinos, give them original names, and put them together in a book. Either way, they are free to imagine dinos in all colors and give them original names.

WHAT THEY LEARN. Much of the material on dinosaurs lends itself to good reading and classifying, and meaningful math for early years kids. Unlike preschoolers who are caught up with the "monster" play aspect of dinos; early school years kids find the science and information surrounding dinosaurs worth digging into.

Read It!

I Spy School Days

(by Jean Marzollo/illus. by Walter Wick, Scholastic) It's great fun to hunt for visual answers to the riddles hidden in the colorful photos. Chock-full of many details, each double page spread has its own theme. One of a magnificent series of books that both adults and children can enjoy puzzling over together. Don't be surprised if your child finds the details before you do! 6–10.

Play It!

Bake a Number — Math/Kitchen Science

Baking requires numbers in so many ways—recipes call for measuring, timing, and temperature. Young bakers will also enjoy baking their numbers (or letters). Use a sugar cookie recipe or premade mix. Instead of rolling the cookies and cutting them out, have your child roll the dough into long "snakes" and shape these into numerals or letters. Have your child bake his age, your telephone number, his name or initials.

WHAT THEY LEARN. Shaping and "writing" with dough gives kids a chance to get the feel for the shape and direction of the numerals and letters. They taste good, too.

MATH

Domino Cookies

Use a sugar cookie dough to make rolled cookies. Cut out several rectangles and score each in the middle like a domino. Use raisins or mini M&Ms to represent the domino dots. Here's the trick. How may ways can your child show his age in dots on the dominoes? Make domino cookies for a friend or sibling who is younger or older.

Give Me a Rhyme, I'll Give You a Dime — Language

Collect several objects from the bottom of a drawer or toy box. Put four or five in plain view. Say you have a key, pen, toy car, and top on the table. Say, "I'm thinking of some thing that rhymes with jar or star." Your child should find the car. Make it a little harder: say, "I'm thinking of something that turns (could be the top or key), made of metal (top or key), and rhymes with tea, or bee...." Players should alternate between being the riddle giver and the riddle solver. Start with 10 dimes in the "kitty." Players take a dime for each riddle they solve or for any riddle that stumps the other player.

WHAT THEY LEARN. Rhyming helps children make generalizations about words in word families—something that makes beginning spelling and reading a lot easier.

Read It!

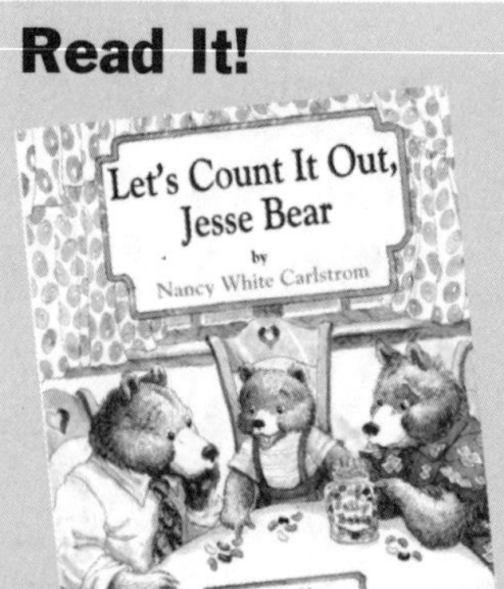

Let's Count It Out, Jesse Bear
(by Nancy White Carlstrom/illus. by Bruce Degen, Simon & Schuster) Lilting rhymes and lovable bouncy Jesse Bear go on a numerical romp from one to twenty, with verse for each number plus a playful intro to adding one more. Does your preschooler know what we mean by one more? (Certainly not, at least if we're talking about cookies!) But try this jumping game to give meaning to one more. 3–6.

Play It!

Jump & Count! **Math**

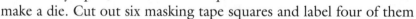

You'll need:

- chalk to make a "ladder" (indoors, use strips of tape)
- a block or box to turn into a die
- red and green construction paper or paint

Step 1. Use any square block or small square box to make a die. Cut out six masking tape squares and label four of them "go" and two of them "stop." Or use any square block or box to make a die and tape four green construction-paper circles (or paint circles) with a big "go" on each; tape or paint two red circles with a "stop" on each.

Step 2. Use chalk to mark a long ladder-shaped grid on the sidewalk with

MATH

numbers from 1 to 10 or 1 to 20, depending on your child's counting skills.

Step 3. Your child tosses the cube. She goes forward once when she rolls a "go," and doesn't move when she rolls a "stop." How many tries does it take to get to 10?

Variations: Jump & Count Some More

1. Use a drum to beat out how many jumps they can take. Object is for child to go up and down the ladder. You can make this more challenging if child can hop on one foot. Either way, this is an active way to learn about adding.

2. Make the ladder go up to 20 for more experienced math jumpers.

3. Have kids stand at the highest number and jump backwards the number of spaces they roll or hear. A concrete way to experience subtraction!

WHAT THEY LEARN. In "Jump & Count," kids are seeing what number is one more than the one they are standing on and what zero means. "Jump & Count Some More" games call for adding or subtracting one or more.

Read It!

Miss Bindergarten Celebrates the 100th Day

(by Joseph Slate/illus. by Ashley Wolff, Dutton) It's a new day to celebrate! Wait 'til you see how all the children and Miss Bindergarten get ready for the 100th day of school. Kids are sure to be inspired by Miss B's class as they gather their collections of 100 paper chain links, beads, blocks, ants, and more. It's fun to study the big, busy amusing illustrations with their amusing details—for instance, what food would be good enough to enjoy 100 pieces of, without getting sick? 5–8.

Play It!

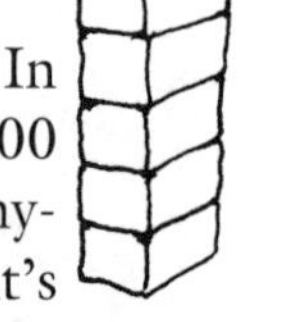

Young school-aged kids love to collect all sorts of things. In the fall they might collect 100 leaves, or how about 100 acorns? 100 seashells? A hundred of anything is a very big number—whether it's pennies, stamps, shells, or buttons. Counting that high may also be challenging. Kids need strategies for keeping track as they build their collections. There are lots of ways to count and sort. Count out 100 plastic blocks or 100 pennies. How can they divide the collection? How many will they have in each stack if they divide them by 2s? 5s? 10s? 20s? 25s? 50s?

MATH

Guess My Pattern Game

Say, "I'm going to count, but not by ones... see if you can guess my pattern and tell what comes next. Listen: 2, 4, 6, 8... what comes next?" Children who are ready for this game love figuring out the simple patterns. A good game to play while you're travelling, or in a waiting room.

Variation

Experienced players can do some patterns in reverse: "14, 12, 10... what comes next?"

Hidden Numbers Game

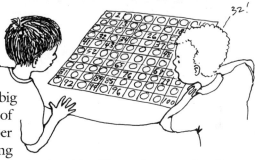

Use pennies or polka chips to cover the numerals from 1 to 100 on a playing board you have made with a big piece of poster board or a large sheet of paper. Players take turns saying a number that the other player must find by picking up the right chip. If they get it right, they take the chip. If not, they put the chip back. Now it is the next player's turn to call a number for the other player to find.

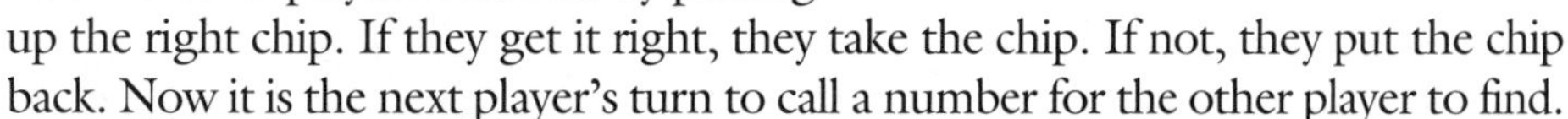

Variation

Make number cards that players take turns drawing and finding the number shown.

WHAT THEY LEARN. Beginners may simply try to guess and lift any chip when they begin to play this game. But before long, they begin to see the patterns of our number system and start to use the clues of the uncovered numbers to find the one they are trying to find.

Read It!

One Lonely Sea Horse

(by Saxton Freymann/illus. by Joost Elffers, Scholastic) Using witty photos of fruits and veggies to represent underwater creatures, this is an entertaining counting book written in rhythmic rhymes. No guarantees that this will promote healthy eating, but it's a good place to start! 3–8.

Play It!

Finger Writing

Writing numerals in flour or sand gives children a chance to shape their numerals or letters with their fingers, instead of having to hold a writing tool. That kind of direct, tactile experience reinforces the shapes of the numerals. Mistakes are easy to erase and there are no lines to stay between. Use a large roasting pan with sides to keep the flour inside. *Variations:* Sometimes writing letters or numerals in the air helps them to practice before putting their hand in the flour. Reinforce direction of numerals by writing a number with your finger on the child's back. No tickling allowed!

Make a Number — Math & Art

Making the dough is easy and great fun. Once the dough is made, give kids plenty of time to explore ways to make their own creations. You can also demonstrate how to make long snakes that they can shape into numerals. Dough will air-harden and can be painted.

Recipe for Dough

Mix together 1 cup of flour, a half cup of salt, a few drops of vegetable oil, and enough water to form a pliable dough. Kids love to get their hands into this squishy mix. Add water slowly and if dough gets too sticky, add flour and a bit more salt to make it dryer. Add a splash of tempera paint, or kids can paint the white dough after it hardens.

Stamp a Counting Book — Math

Children love to make simple books that they can "read." Use tempera paint in dishes and cut out some geometric shapes from a sponge. Let them experiment with the stamp art to make their own creations. Then suggest making a counting book. You can print the numeral and number word on each page. Have the child stamp the matching number of shapes on each page. Staple the book together and it's ready for "reading." A good way to learn about sequencing as well as counting.

Veggie Critters — Art

Take inspiration from the amusing photographs in the book. For lunch or a tea party, use veggies to make interesting critters that children can design with a little adult help. Let the shapes of the veggies "speak" to you and look for edible add-ons that can be used for making features. Pitted olives sliced in rings make good eyes, half a cherry tomato makes a funny nose—both can be attached with cream cheese or toothpicks.

WHAT THEY LEARN. Playing around with numbers is the best way to give children a sense of mastery. Find informal ways to use and notice numbers when you go walking up steps, dial the phone, or set the table. These informal moments are the best way to develop a math-wise child.

Read It!

The Three Bears

(retold by Byron Barton, HarperCollins) What children's library would be complete without this classic? There's a clear and repetitive framework and suspense in this timeless story. Reissued in sturdy cardboard, there's no better concept book for introducing such basics as size comparisons and simple counting. 2½ & up.

Play It!

Big, Medium, and Small Game — Math & Active Play

Reinforce the size concepts from the story with three boxes—a big box, a medium box, and a small box (of course). Use a line of tape to mark where players stand and take turns tossing a beanbag or small bear into the boxes. Is it easier to get the beanbag in the big box or the small box? Put a number 1 on the big box, 2 on the medium box, and 3 on the small box. Keep score with chips, pretzels, or raisins, which players take when they get one into the box. Winner is the first to get ten chips.

WHAT THEY LEARN. Active games help kids develop their throwing arm and eye/hand coordination, and build understanding of size concepts by using hands-on, concrete materials.

Bears in Chairs — Pretend Play

Have a Three Bears Porridge breakfast or Three Bears Soup lunch. Help your child find a big teddy bear, a middle-sized bear, and a wee little baby bear (or dolls will do). Set the table with three sizes of bowls; fill your child's bowl with real cereal, and pretend to fill the other bowls. Setting the scene with props helps kids make the leap to pretend.

Retell It! — Language

Most older preschoolers have been hearing this story since they were toddlers. Now your preschooler will enjoy retelling the story to you. Let her begin with the pictures to guide the telling. The object is not to use the words in the book, but to encourage your child to tell it in her own words. Eventually, your child will be able to tell the tale without the book, by using her memory and pictures in the mind's eye. Using dolls to act out the story, or dictating the story into a tape recorder also motivate kids to tell this and other favorite tales.

Try other printed versions of the story, too, so your child can see how adults have retold it in their own words. For an especially warm and fuzzy retelling with charming illustrations, see Valeri Gorbachev's (North-South Books).

WHAT THEY LEARN. Retelling a story calls for putting a story in their own words, recalling a sequence of events, and understanding that a story has a beginning, middle, and end. These are skills that readers will need for comprehension.

Read It!

Twelve Hats for Lena

(by Karen Katz, McElderry Books) Suppose you could make a hat for each month of the year. What would you put on each one to reflect the season or important holiday? Done in charming collage with gouache and colored pencils, this is a book that will inspire young artists as well as introduce them to the names of the months of the year. 3–8.

Play It!

Calendar Math

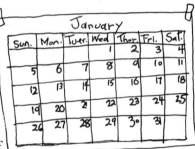

Kids have such busy schedules—what with lessons, meetings, play dates, and parties—that knowing the months of the year and days of the week is no small item! It helps to have a calendar hanging where the important events of each day can be seen in a glance.

- Help your child make a blank calendar grid by hand or on the computer. Leave enough space in the daily boxes to mark events legibly.
- School-age kids will be able to write the numerals.
- Kids can add stickers or drawings to mark special events such as holidays and birthdays.
- Children can keep track of the weather by adding

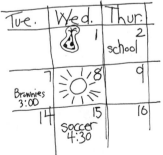

symbols for sunny, rainy, or cloudy days.

- With first and second graders, play a date game—“I’m thinking of the first Wednesday in November—what will the date be?”

WHAT THEY LEARN. Young children don’t have a full understanding of time. So when a parent goes on a trip or a big event is near, a calendar can help make abstract concepts of time more concrete and understandable. Using blank calendars help kids discover that day “1” of the month may start on different days of the week. Filling in the numbers gives practice in writing and a first-hand understanding of how calendars work.

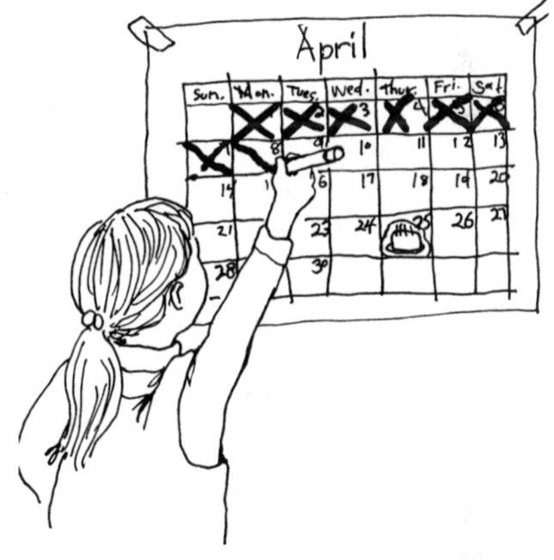

Calendar Art to Hang or Wear

Use seasonal gift wraps, old greeting cards, and cutouts from magazines, plus found trims such as ribbons, doilies, or stickers to make collages to decorate the calendar each month. Or celebrate the first of each month with a new hat. Use the same collage materials to paste to hats as shown in *Joseph Had a Little Overcoat* (p. 18).

Read It!

Blueberries for Sal

(by Robert McCloskey, Viking) When Little Sal and her mom go to Blueberry Hill to pick berries, Sal wanders off; on the other side of the hill, Little Bear does the same. It's the sound of the berries in the pail going "kuplink, kuplank, kuplunk" that startles Little Bear's mother, who rushes off to find her little one. All's well that ends well in this suspenseful tale that has been loved by generations of young children. 3–6.

Play It!

Kuplink, Kuplank, Kuplunk! — Math

Play a little listening game. Player 1 needs an empty pot and some small building blocks. Player 2 needs a spoon and a pot. How you play: Player 2 taps her pot one to five times. Player 1 must drop one to five blocks, one at a time, into the pot, making the same number of kuplunks that Player 2 tapped. Learning to listen is fun when you turn it into a game. Switch roles so both players get to kuplunk and tap.

Blueberry Muffins — Kitchen Science

Little Sal didn't save many berries to bring home, but her mom did. How about making some yummy blueberry muffins? This is a fun parent/child project. You can use a mix from the supermarket, to which you add fresh blueberries, or work from scratch with a simple recipe for twelve blueberry muffins:

Preheat oven to 400°. Grease muffin tin.

You'll need:

- 2 cups sifted flour
- 2 tablespoons of sugar
- 2½ teaspoons baking powder
- ½ teaspoon salt
- 1 beaten egg
- 1 cup of milk
- 4 tablespoons of melted butter or margarine
- 1 cup of blueberries

Sift the dry ingredients together. Mix the milk, egg, and butter. Now mix the liquid and dry ingredients. Mix only until the flour is moist, but not smooth. Add the blueberries. Fill muffin tins about two-thirds full. Bake for 25 minutes.

WHAT THEY LEARN. Measuring and mixing the ingredients makes real connections among all the ways we use numbers in real life. It helps kids understand that everything does not come ready-made. Talk about how the flour changes from dry and powdery to moist and sticky when it's blended with other ingredients. Then talk about how the wet batter changes in baking. Cooking provides many opportunities to give meaning to language, and grow kids' language as well as their math skills.

Read It!

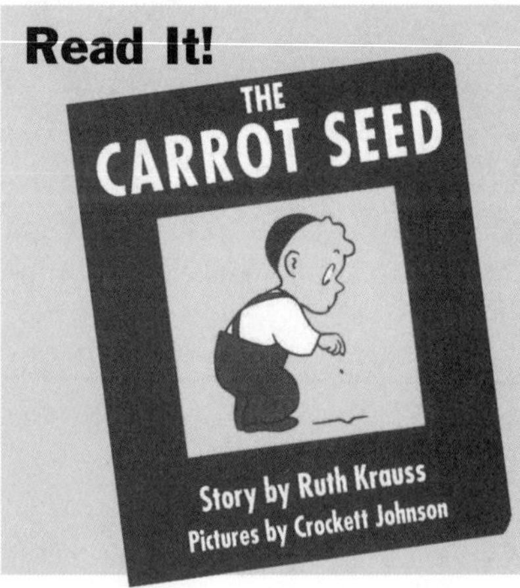

The Carrot Seed
(by Ruth Kraus/illus. by Crockett Johnson, HarperCollins) A small boy plants a carrot seed that everyone tells him will never grow. But faith springs eternal and, ultimately, so does the carrot! This small story about a stubborn optimist has pleased generations of little gardeners. 4–7.

Play It!

Recycled Grocery Garden   Kitchen Science

You may not be able to grow an immense carrot like the one in this story, but you can do something almost as magical! Take photos of this experiment or have your child make pictures of the changes. Write simple captions that your child dictates or writes to describe what is happening. Keep the log in a notebook or small photo flip book that will become a book they will enjoy rereading.

Step 1. Cut about an inch off the top of fresh carrots, turnips or beets that still have some short green stems showing.

Step 2. Put the veggie tops in a shallow dish or bowl with about a quarter inch of water. Put them in a sunny window where your child can watch

them. Keep them moist and in a few days you will begin to see sprouts growing out of the carrot tops.

Step 3. Before long there will be a forest of green leafy "carrot trees."

Step 4. Add some miniature animals—ready-made or homemade of clay—and put them on pebbles that keep them out of the water in the forest. Now your child can make up his own carrot forest story.

VARIATIONS: Other foods you can recycle & grow

AVOCADO PIT

SWEET POTATO VINE

POT-A-TOP OF PINEAPPLE

WHAT THEY LEARN. Using seeds, roots, and cuttings enlarges a child's view of how different plants grow. This kind of windowsill garden is scaled to size for beginning gardeners. Keeping a pictorial log also gives them a small, do-able writing/dictating task that results in a book they can add to their personal library.

Read It!

Do Monkeys Tweet?

(by Melanie Walsh, Houghton Mifflin) Do dogs oink? Do horses bark? Preschoolers will giggle smugly at the totally ridiculous questions and gloat at how smart they are because they know the names of the animals that tweet, bark, oink, or... whatever, on the turn page. From the author of the equally delightful *Do Pigs Have Stripes?* 3–5.

Play It!

Jump and Shout! **Science & Language**

Play this active listening game with a group or one child.

Step 1. Start the game with players sitting.

Step 2. Make up your own ridiculous statements about animals and what they do, what sounds they make, or how they look.

Step 3. Preschoolers listen and sit still as you say some true facts, for example: "cows

moo," "dogs bark." BUT they have to jump when you say something silly such as "cats crow," or "elephants have stripes."

Variation: Older children will like switching roles and making up true and untrue statements about animals.

WHAT THEY LEARN. Preschoolers need to listen carefully as you speak in order to know when to jump. This is an active and entertaining way to help them learn to listen, think, and respond. They will relish how smart they are while they jump to your silly statements. Their upside-down brand of humor also comes into play with the fun of hearing or making up silly statements.

Guess My Animal Game

Line up a row of four stuffed animals. Have your child turn around as you take one of the animals away. Have child look again and tell which animal is missing. Variation: Leave all four animals, but change the position of two. Can your child tell which ones were moved? A fun way to develop your child's observation skills and visual memory.

Read It!

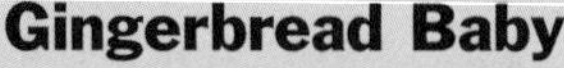

Gingerbread Baby

(by Jan Brett, Putnam) Here's a kinder, gentler telling of the traditional Gingerbread Boy. Matti and his mom pop a gingerbread man into the oven. But when Matti opens the oven door too soon, out comes the Gingerbread Baby, who runs out shouting the well-known refrain, "Catch me if you can!" While everyone chases after the gingerbread baby, Matti is seen making a perfect place for his gingerbread friend. This is one version where the fox is outfoxed. 3–7.

Play It!

Easy Gingerbread Houses — Kitchen Science

Make a village of Gingerbread Houses, rather than one big house. Children can help mix and roll the dough and assemble the houses or, for younger children, you pre-bake and pre-assemble houses and have children do the decorating.

Step 1. Mix and chill the dough according to the cookie recipe on the box or your favorite recipe. The big trick is to keep the dough cold. Work on one house at a time and leave the rest of the dough in the fridge. While the dough is chilling, make the templates.

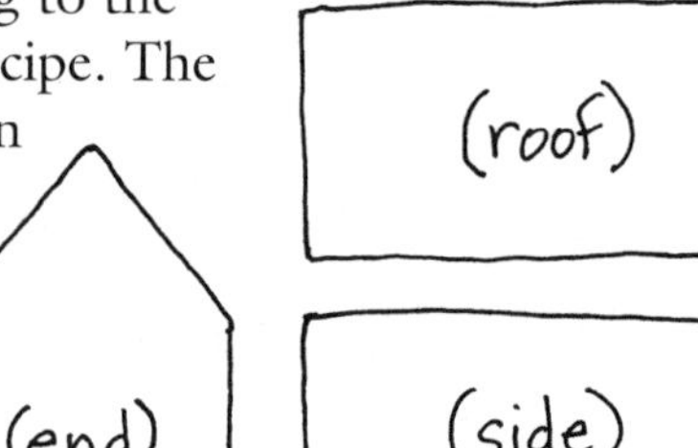

Step 2. Draw three templates like the ones at right (but larger) and cut them out of cardboard.

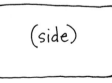

Step 3. Check templates to make sure that they line up and will fit together.

Step 4. Roll out the dough. Trace a double set of the templates on the dough, cut, and bake. (You should have two pointed walls, two rectangular walls, and two roof pieces.)

Step 5. Once the pieces have cooled, put the house together using "sugar glue" as "cement." You'll have to hold the glued walls together until they set.

Note: Royale frosting recipes use raw egg whites and pose a health hazard. Instead, we suggest mixing confectioner's sugar and water into a glue-like substance (see page 34).

A Little Math Puzzle — Math

Have your school-aged child help figure these out:

- If one package of gingerbread mix will make enough dough for two small houses, how many mixes will you need for six houses?
- You'll need approximately 20 pieces of candy to trim each house. How many pieces will you need to decorate six houses? ten houses? Have your child help divvy up the candy (tasting allowed for helpers) and put it on plates in front of each decorating station.

Gingerbread People — Art

Use the same mix or recipe to create a cast of gingerbread boys, girls, and creatures. Do not open the oven too soon, or one may hop out! Cool and decorate with icing in tubes, and raisins or candies. By the way, how do you eat your gingerbread—from the head down, or the toes up?

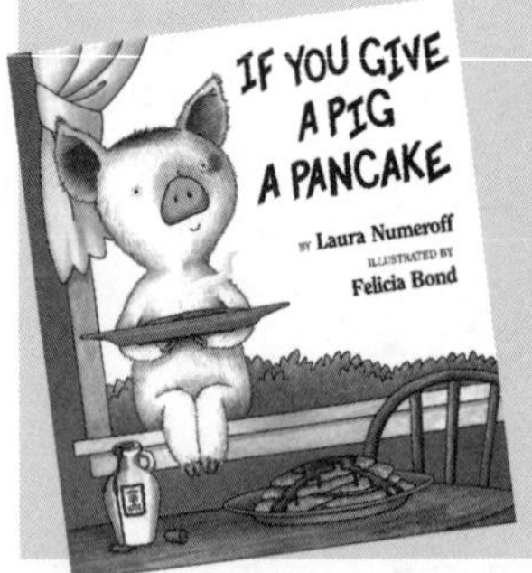

If You Give a Pig a Pancake
(by Laura Numeroff/illus. by Felicia Bond, HarperCollins) If you read this book to your kids, they are sure to want pancakes. If you make pancakes with your kids, they're sure to have fun... and they can also have a small science experience if you talk about how things change as your child helps to mix the batter. 3–6.

Play It!

Silver Dollar Pancakes — Kitchen Science

Step 1. Use a pancake mix or make the batter from scratch. You will have to help with the measuring and mixing. Talk about how the dry flour mixed with the milk becomes a liquid that you can pour.

Step 2. Kids can help with pouring the liquid if you put it into a measuring cup with a pouring lip. Or use a squeeze bottle to squeeze the batter out into small silver-dollar-size pancakes.

Step 3. Add syrup and butter, and enjoy!

Homemade Butter — Kitchen Science

If you make pancakes, you'll need butter. Here's an easy way to make it.

You'll need:
- pint of heavy cream
- a jar with a good lid
- a strong arm

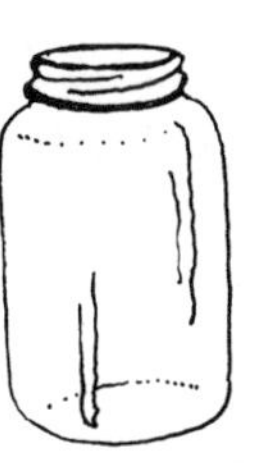

Step 1. Put a pint of heavy cream in a jar. Fasten lid firmly.

Step 2. Start shaking—the jar, that is.

Step 3. It takes lots of time so you will need to take turns. Set a timer for five minutes. When the timer rings, pass the jar to another shaker. Meanwhile, sing a little shaking song:

"Shake, shake, shake... Make some butter!"

Step 4. Spread on pancakes (or toast) and enjoy!

*How many five-minute turns will it take?

"If I Say..." Game & Book — Language & Art

This is a fun word association/thinking game for a case of waiting-room or back-seat blues. You start by saying, "I'm going to say a word and you tell me something that goes with it." Give a simple example:

"If I say salt, you'll probably say... pepper."
"If I say peanut butter, you'll say..."
"If I say toast, you'll say..."

After you've played this game, it's fun for kids to make a book of their own by drawing pictures of things that go together.

Read It!

Jack and the Beanstalk

(retold by Steven Kellogg, William Morrow) Jack's magic beans sprout into a beanstalk that takes Jack on his great adventure. While it's full of the usual suspense and danger, Kellogg's illustrations add a special and memorable flavor to this classic tale. Save this one for school-aged kids, who will relish the scary parts and Jack's triumph! 5–8.

Play It!

Racing Vines

You may not be able to grow a beanstalk that will reach up to the land of giants, but beans do sprout with an almost overnight magic about them. Kids will be amazed by doing a variety of window garden bean plantings that have more science than fantasy about them.

You'll need:

- dried beans—lima beans are perfect, even if you have no potting soil!
- paper towels
- clear plastic jars or glasses
- water

Step 1. Have your child moisten a paper towel and scrunch it into a glass.

Step 2. Put a few lima bean seeds between the paper and around the side of the glass so he can see the seeds.

Step 3. Put the glass in a sunny window and keep the paper moist (not soaked) and observe what happens.

Step 4. Try the same experiment but put the second glass in a dark place and watch what happens. You can transplant the seeds into soil or start others in a pot and grow a beanstalk.

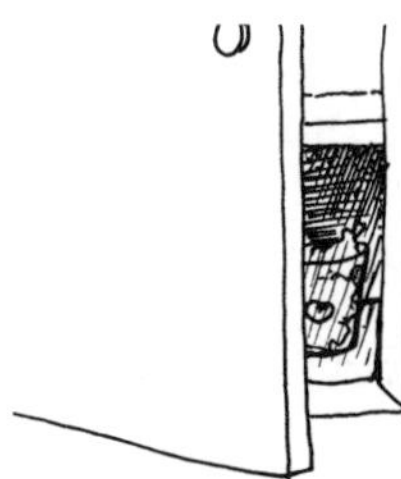

WHAT THEY LEARN. Inside of a seed is a baby plant just waiting to grow. Talk about what the seed needed to get started. In the summer months plant string beans for an almost-sure-to-succeed bean crop. Even chronic veggie haters can't resist eating their own home-grown beans.

Retell It!

Language

Jack does take quite a few things from the Giant's house. Suppose that you were the Giant's wife, the Harp, the Hen, or the Giant reporting the "crime" to the police. Use puppets or pretend to be reporting about the incident on TV. Have one person play the interviewer and the other play a character from the story. Role-playing gives kids an opportunity to see that there is usually more than one side to a story.

Read It!

The Maestro Plays

(by Bill Martin/illus. by Vladimir Radunsky, Holt) Catchy rhythm, rhyme and sprightly bright cut paper illustrations orchestrate a playful collection of instruments that the Maestro uses to make music. An entertaining way to introduce children to the instruments of the orchestra. 2–5.

Play It!

Shake & Strum Fun — Science & Art

Children love to create and use their own instruments from found material. Here are some classics:

Box Banjo. Use crayons or paints to decorate a shoe box. Stretch rubber bands of varying thicknesses around the box. Talk about which bands make the highest sound. Which are lowest?

Rhythm Shakers. Use stickers or paints to decorate metal Band-Aid boxes or plastic deli containers to make terrific shakers. Experiment with various fillings for different sounds—try pebbles, rice, Cheerios. Tape the box shut. Talk about words that describe the sounds each of the varying fillings makes.

Fill & Spill Water Xylophone. Make a tinkling musical instrument by filling eight glasses or jars with varying heights of water. Hit the glasses with a spoon.

Fill and spill until you can play a musical scale. Talk about which glasses make the high sounds and which make the low sounds? What would happen if you added another glass with more water? Write down your child's prediction and then test it. (Adult supervision required with glass.)

Drums. (See *Max Found Two Sticks,* page 40).

Pretend Play/Musical Activity **Active Play**

Maestro. Who wouldn't love becoming the maestro? Find a safe but suitable "baton," such as a paper towel tube or a plastic straw, and let the music begin. Play recordings of music with distinctive rhythms such as marches or symphonic music, and encourage your child to conduct like the maestro or play along with homemade instruments.

Freeze/Melt Game. Use the rhythm shakers or a drum for this active movement game. Play the shakers as your child moves until the shakers stop when they must freeze like an ice statue in whatever position they are caught in.

WHAT THEY LEARN. Making and using musical instruments involves both little fingers and big motor muscles. These activities involve a bit of science, art, listening, moving, and lots of fun.

Read It!

The Magic School Bus Explores the Senses

(by Joanna Cole/illus. by Bruce Degen, Scholastic) Ms. Frizzle's class is off on another adventure. This time Mr. Wilde, the new assistant principal, takes the wheel and races to catch Ms. Frizzle with an important message. There's lots of excitement as the class explores the senses travelling through the eye of a police officer, a boy's ear, a dog's nose, and onto Ms. Frizzle's tongue. 5–8.

Play It!

Guessing Scents — Science

You'll need:

- ten small paper cups
- aluminum foil
- a pencil
- various scented materials

Make five pairs of cups, each with a matching pair of scents. For example, cinnamon, tea bags, strawberries, garlic powder, lemon juice all work well. (You can place a damp paper towel in the cup and sprinkle a spice on top.) Cover with foil and punch enough holes in the top so that you can smell what's inside. Place all ten cups in front of the first player. How quickly can they put the cups in pairs? A good rainy day activity.

Magic Number Trick — Math

Step 1. Cut up four equal size pieces of paper.

Step 2. Print the even numbers 2, 4, 6, 8 on one side.

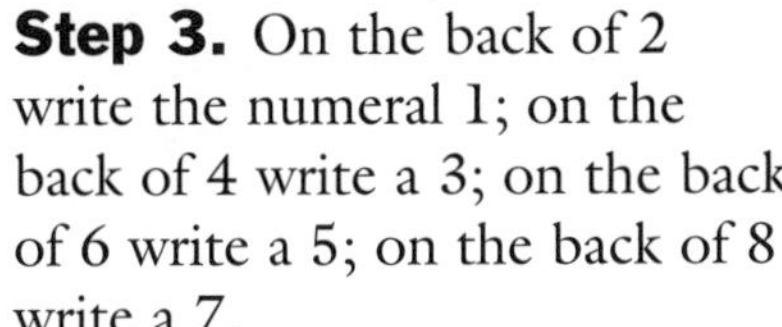

Step 3. On the back of 2 write the numeral 1; on the back of 4 write a 3; on the back of 6 write a 5; on the back of 8 write a 7.

Step 4. Now give the cards to a friend and let her examine them. Say, "I'm going to put these cards down and I will ask you to turn one card over. Before you do it, I am going to write a number on this piece of paper." Without showing her the number, write 17 on your paper and fold it. Say, "You will say this number!"

Step 5. Now put the cards down with all the odd numbers showing. Tell your friend to turn any card over and add the four numbers. Her answer will always be 17.

Variation: Put the cards down with the even numbers showing and write down the number 19. Have your friend turn any card over and the answer will match yours! Can you tell why?

Read It!

Martha Blah Blah

(by Susan Meddaugh, Houghton Mifflin) Martha, that clever talking dog who learned to speak after eating alphabet soup, is having a language problem! In this funny sequel, Martha gets caught in an economy squeeze, but uses her nose to solve the mystery and regain her special power! Don't miss Meddaugh's other award winners: *Martha Speaks, Martha Calling,* and *Martha & Skits.* 4–8.

Play It!

Martha Blah Blah Soup! **Kitchen Science**

Many kids think that soup comes only in cans. It often does, but making soup from scratch is amazingly simple and special—especially if it has alphabet noodles. Children can really help in the process and learn a lot about following directions, measuring, and transforming a collection of ingredients into tasty soup. Here's how you do it:

You'll need:

- 4–6 cups of water
- 1–2 bouillon cubes (vegetable or chicken)
- 1 piece of celery
- 1 onion, cut up
- 2 carrots, cut up, and any other veggies in the bin (optional)
- Salt & pepper
- Alphabet noodles

Step 1. Have kids wash the veggies and measure and pour the cold water into the pot.

Step 2. Add the bouillon cubes and stir until they dissolve.

Step 3. Add the cut-up celery, a small onion, a carrot, salt and pepper to the pot. Bring it to a boil and then turn down to a simmer.

Step 4. Simmer until the veggies are tender. Taste and adjust seasoning to taste.

Step 5. In another pot, bring water to boil and add alphabet noodles. Cook until tender, drain and add to soup along with chunks of chicken (optional).

Step 6. Get ready to Blah! Blah! Blah!

WHAT THEY LEARN. Cooking calls for using school-related skills such as reading, measuring, and working in a step-by-step sequence.

Write It! Act It!

Interview with Martha

Have your child pretend that he is a reporter and can interview the world-famous dog. What questions would he ask Martha about herself, her canine friends and family? About her adventures? Her favorite food—other than alphabet soup?

Write down the questions that your school-aged child would ask Martha. Next, either have your child write the answers as if she were Martha, or use them for an interview as if you were on a radio/TV talk show. You play the host and have your child pretend to be Martha.

Read It!

Mouse Paint

(by Ellen Stoll Walsh, Harcourt) Three little white mice get into some paint, and the results stir up a playful demonstration of how colors are mixed. Reading about it is fun, but doing it is even better! 3–6.

Play It!

As the mice do in *Mouse Paint,* there are many ways for kids to experiment with mixing colors. Here are several ways to stir up some colorful fun!

Hot Air Painting — Science & Art

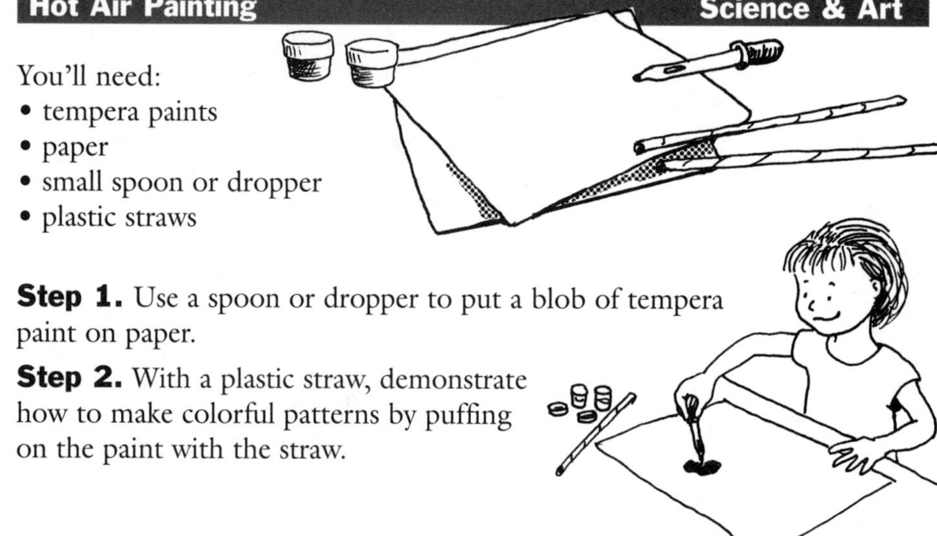

You'll need:

- tempera paints
- paper
- small spoon or dropper
- plastic straws

Step 1. Use a spoon or dropper to put a blob of tempera paint on paper.

Step 2. With a plastic straw, demonstrate how to make colorful patterns by puffing on the paint with the straw.

Step 3. Add a second color and *shazammmm!* You make a new color!

Use these designs for place mats or larger sheets to make colorful and unique wrapping paper.

String Painting — Art

You'll need:

- red, yellow, and blue tempera paint
- big pieces of paper
- pieces of string 8–10 inches; try string and yarn of different thicknesses
- three paper plates
- newspapers

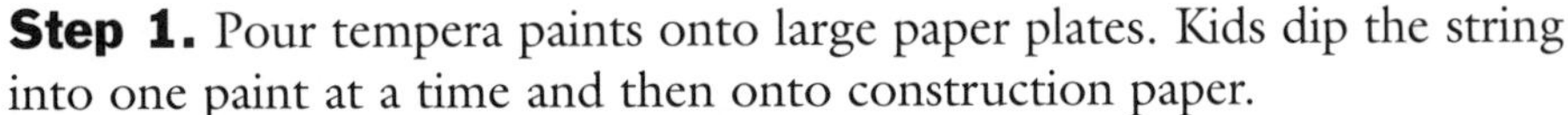

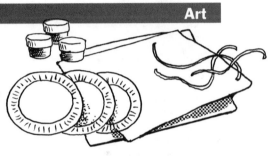

Step 1. Pour tempera paints onto large paper plates. Kids dip the string into one paint at a time and then onto construction paper.

Step 2. Try moving the string around or put it down in a squiggly design and then lift it up. By using another string, they can introduce a second color that may even blend to produce a third color.

WHAT THEY LEARN. These are playful ways to experiment with mixing colors. There's no expectation here for making a "picture" of something. So this is an art experience that focuses on color exploration for its own sake.

Read It!

Raising Dragons

(by Jerdine Nolen/illus. by Elise Primavera, Harcourt) Pa and Ma don't really approve of having a dragon around when their daughter finds a giant egg that hatches. But in this delightful fantasy, that dragon manages to do more good than harm. Like most tales of a "boy and his dog," this bond between a girl and her dragon must come to an end. In this case, the end of one relationship is ripe with a multitude of other possibilities. 5–8.

Play It!

Egg Magic Trick

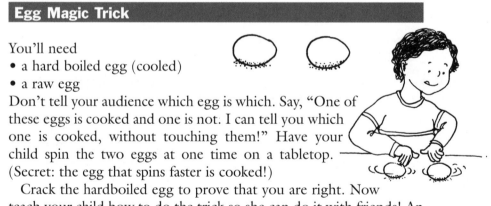

You'll need

- a hard boiled egg (cooled)
- a raw egg

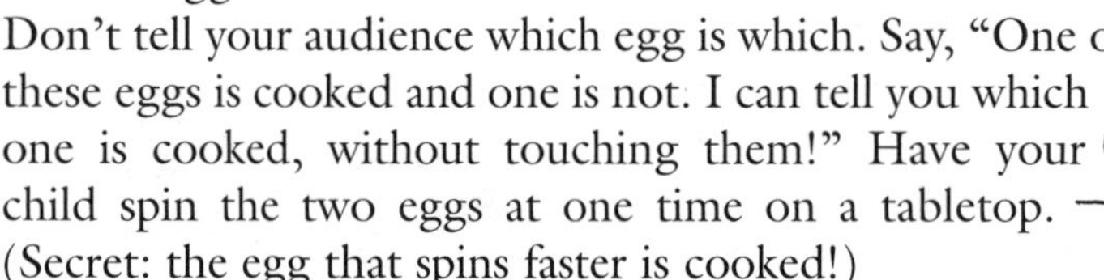

Don't tell your audience which egg is which. Say, "One of these eggs is cooked and one is not. I can tell you which one is cooked, without touching them!" Have your child spin the two eggs at one time on a tabletop. (Secret: the egg that spins faster is cooked!)

Crack the hardboiled egg to prove that you are right. Now teach your child how to do the trick so she can do it with friends! An early physics lesson.

An Egg-Citing Game:

How many creatures can you name that hatch from an egg? Can you and your child put at least five creatures under each heading (below)? If not, check the encyclopedia together!

WHAT THEY LEARN. This game extends the idea of what hatches from an egg while developing their ability to classify.

Birds	**Reptiles**	**Amphibians**	**Fish**	**Insects**

Resist Wax Eggs — Art

Cut egg shapes out of paper and have child use light-colored crayons to make a picture or design on the egg. Now put some watered-down tempera paint in a dish. When the paint is applied to the egg, the crayon designs will still appear.

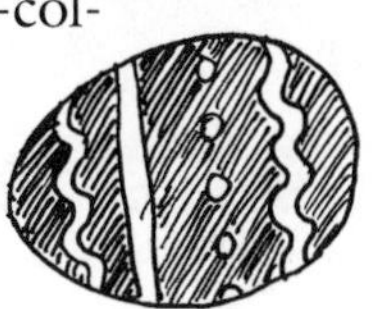

Clay Dragons — Art & Language

When the dragon has finished its work and is returned to its native island, the young heroine is given a gift. She returns home with new dragon eggs. What kinds of dragons do your children think will hatch from the new eggs? What will these dragon hatchlings be able to do?

After reading the story, encourage kids use paint, crayons, or clay to show what the new dragons will look like and give their hatchlings names. Some children may be inspired to tell or write a new adventure!

Read It!

The Snowy Day

(by Ezra Jack Keats, Viking) Here is the excitement of snow as seen through the eyes of a small boy who awakens to a world blanketed in snow. As Peter makes footprints, angels, and snowballs, Keats' collages and words capture the timeless wonderment of it all. You can buy this as a board book, but it's not a book for babies. 2½–6.

Play It!

Snowball Races — Science

Share this on a snowy day and take a page from Peter by bringing home a few snowballs to see what happens.

PUT ONE IN A DISH NEAR A SUNNY WINDOW.

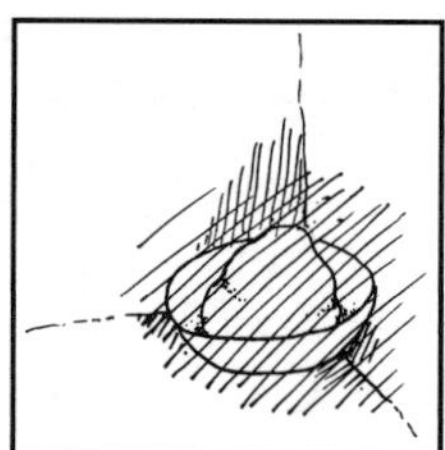

PUT ANOTHER IN A DISH IN A DARK PLACE.

PUT STILL ANOTHER IN THE REFRIGERATOR.

Discuss what your child thinks will happen to the snowballs.

No snow? Try an alternative: freeze some water in several paper cups and test what happens to three different cups in different locations.

What's in the Snow? — Science

Fresh snow has a way of looking pure and clean. But is it? Have your child bring a snowball inside and let it melt in a clear glass or place it in a coffee filter paper. Observe melted snow with a magnifying glass. After seeing the dirt that is usually visible in melted snow kids can better understand why tasting snow is not so great an idea.

WHAT THEY LEARN. A great opportunity for kids to make hypotheses and test them out in relatively short time—before they lose interest. Taking photos at each stage will turn this into a book kids will enjoy revisiting even when winter is gone.

Draw It!

Wet Chalk Painting — Art

Dip dark construction paper in water and give your child white chalk for making Snowy Day paintings. (Put something under the paper since the colored paper will stain a tabletop.)

Cook It!

Use a toothpick and vegetable coloring to "draw" eyes, nose and mouths on marshmallows and float them in a cup of hot chocolate when you come in from the snow. It's fun to watch the marshmallow face spread as it melts.

Read It!

Strega Nona

(by Tomie dePaola, Putnam) The kindly, grandmotherly witch leaves her bumbling assistant, Big Anthony, to take care of her house. He has been warned not to touch Strega Nona's magic pasta pot, but he does not listen. Nor does the pot. Big Anthony knows how to get it to make pasta—but not how to stop it! 4–8.

Play It!

Pass the Pasta **Kitchen Science**

You may not have a magic pot, but for kids, cooking pasta is quite magical.

You'll need:

- pasta
- a measuring cup
- a pot of boiling water

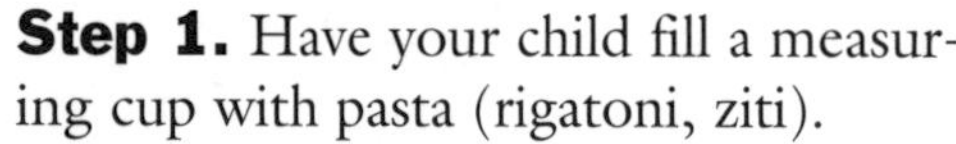

Step 1. Have your child fill a measuring cup with pasta (rigatoni, ziti).

Step 2. Ask him if he thinks all the pasta will fit back into the same cup once it's cooked.

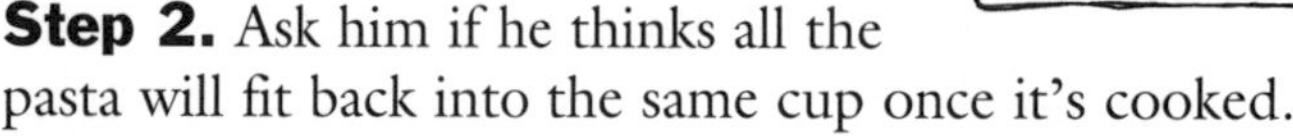

Step 3. Cook the pasta and rinse it with cool water as you drain it.

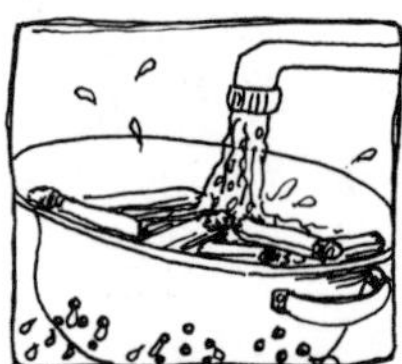

Step 4. Once it's cooked, fill the measuring cup with cooked pasta. Does it all fit? What's happened? Welcome their theories.

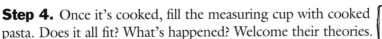

Step 5. Add butter, cheese, sauce, or whatever, and *mangia!*

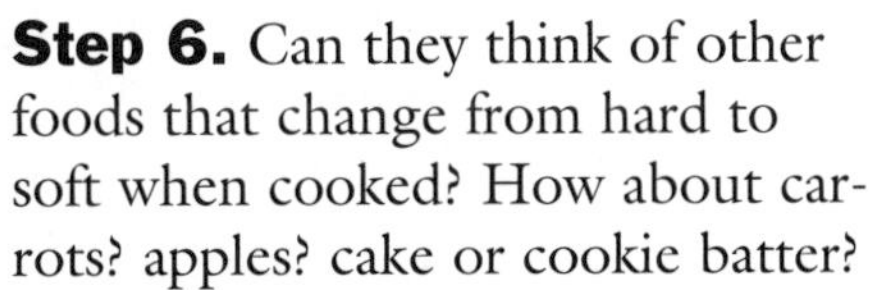

Step 6. Can they think of other foods that change from hard to soft when cooked? How about carrots? apples? cake or cookie batter?

WHAT THEY LEARN. Seeing how the hard pasta changes its texture is interesting, but not nearly as amazing as seeing how the pasta expands. Talk about their theories of why all the pasta won't fit in the cup. Forming their own hypotheses is as much a part of the learning as the answer. Compare the hard pasta to a hard dry sponge that expands when it absorbs water. A tasty science lesson that needs a little butter or sauce!

Witch Hunt — Active Game/Listening

Big Anthony probably couldn't play this listening game very well. But most kids like listening for these kinds of directions. Learning to use the information they get is part of the fun.

Step 1. Cut out a witch's hat with construction paper, or dress a doll as a witch.

Step 2. Have one child who is "It" leave the room while another child hides the witch as everyone else watches.

Step 3. Have "It" return to hunt for the witch. All the children help her find the witch by calling out, "You're getting warm!" as "It" gets closer or, "You're getting cold!" as "It" gets farther from the witch. "It" gets to hide the witch on the next round and chooses the child to become the next "It."

Read It!

Sylvester and the Magic Pebble
(by William Steig, Simon & Schuster) Young Sylvester finds a magic pebble that grants him one wish too many. Poor Sylvester gets locked in a big stone until his devoted parents ultimately free him. A not-to-be-missed classic that speaks about love and interdependence. 4–8.

Play It!

Paperweight or Doorstop — Art

After hearing Sylvester's tale, kids may not be so eager to own a magic pebble for wishing. But one special rock could be a terrific paperweight to keep on a desk or, if it is big enough, a doorstop. It might also be a reminder to be careful what you wish for—you might get it!

You'll need:
- A collection of smooth rocks
- Acrylic paint and brushes

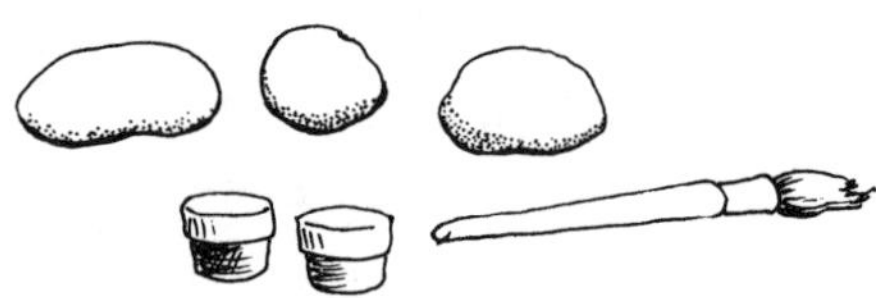

A trip to a beach is likely to turn up the smoothest rocks for painting. But if that's not possible, kids will find special rocks on any walk to a park. Encourage your rock hound to look for some with interesting shapes that suggest the features they add. Some kids may simply like to paint an abstract design with stripes, dots, or zigzags.

Step 1. Clean the rocks and cover a work area where the rocks can be painted and allowed to dry.

Step 2. Use acrylic paints to make a design or transform the rocks into unique creatures.

Sort & Show — Science

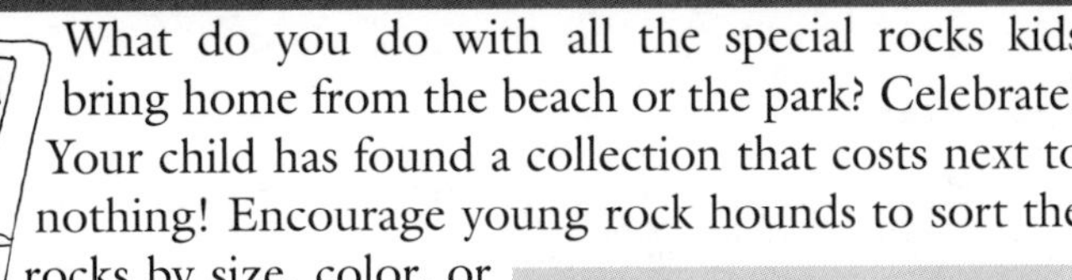

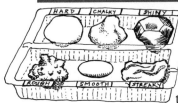

What do you do with all the special rocks kids bring home from the beach or the park? Celebrate! Your child has found a collection that costs next to nothing! Encourage young rock hounds to sort the rocks by size, color, or texture. Older children can use a rock guide to identify the kind of rocks they have found. Will any of the rocks "write" on a sidewalk or driveway?

WHAT THEY LEARN. Starting a rock collection encourages kids to take a closer look and classify them by common attributes. Older kids can look for proper names of rocks in a field guide to rocks. Training the eye to look and compare the details develops visual discrimination as well as language to describe those differences.

Talk About Wishes — Language

Long ago, kids who lived on farms far from the city would put checks on all the things in big catalogs that they called "wish books." If they were lucky, one or two wishes might arrive for a birthday or other holiday. Have you ever made a wish that came true? Did it turn out to be as wonderful as you hoped it would be?

Read It!

The Very Hungry Caterpillar

(by Eric Carle, Putnam) Young preschoolers love the repetition of the text, the subject of eating, and poking their little fingers into all the little holes the hungry caterpillar has eaten through. Packed with so many concepts—colors, days of the week, and an introduction to the big idea of metamorphosis—this is a beauty of a book that will be enjoyed on many levels. 3–5.

Play It!

Now it's your turn! Have a tasting feast, sampling some of the very same fruits the hungry caterpillar ate. As you taste the fruits, talk about how some fruit, such as bananas, are soft, while some fruits, such as apples, are hard and crunchy, and still others, such as watermelons and plums, are watery and drippy.

Fruit Kebob Patterns — Math

You'll need: wooden skewers and fruit chunks

WHAT THEY LEARN. Tasting, feeling, and talking extend your child's way of thinking about fruits with their senses. Preschoolers still learn best through their senses, and tasting parties add meaning to words that help them describe the many things we call fruits.

Use a variety of fruits to make patterned kebobs. Put cut-up chunks on a platter and encourage kids to come up with their own original "patterned" kebobs. Alternate a chunk of banana with a piece of apple to make a pattern: soft/crunchy/

soft/crunchy/soft/crunchy. Patterns can be made with color, texture, size, etc.

Tell Me Game — Science

This classifying game can be played by mixed ages—just agree that younger players need to come up with only three examples, and older players must give five.

Ask kids to tell three or five:

- foods that are green
- foods that are yellow
- vehicles that have two wheels
- animals that swim
- animals that fly
- animals that walk on two legs
- foods that are red
- foods that are orange
- vehicles that have four or more wheels
- animals that walk on four legs

A Room Full of Butterflies — Art

Step 1. Fold a piece of paper in half.

Step 2. Open it and drop a splat of paint in the crease with a dropper or spoon.

Step 3. Add a splat of another color in the crease.

Step 4. Fold the paper again and use your finger tips to spread the paint. Open, and you should find matching splots on each side of the paper.

Step 5. When dry, fold the paper and cut it as if you were making one butterfly wing. Make a batch of butterflies!

Step 6. Use a hole punch and hang on strings in a room with a breeze.

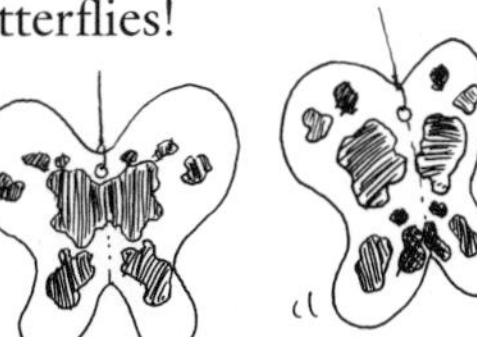

SUBJECT GUIDE

The Table of Contents is organized by the primary activity on the page for each book. Below are other listings that refer you to other topics covered by any given title. Page numbers are in parentheses.

Active Physical Play

Language: Dramatic, Retelling a Story, Memory Games, Comparative Lit

Letter Names & Sounds

Writing

Make a Book

Multicultural

Art

Math: Counting, Patterns, Shapes

Science & Kitchen Science

Baking* & Cooking

Visit our website.

www.toyportfolio.com Updates, reviews of award winners, media listings, and parenting articles.

Are you in a parenting group or play group?

Contact us about special rates available for fundraisers and bulk orders.

Oppenheim Toy Portfolio, Inc.
40 East 9th St., Suite 14M
New York, New York 10003
(212) 598-0502
www.toyportfolio.com

Founded in 1989, the **Oppenheim Toy Portfolio** is the only independent review of children's media. **Joanne Oppenheim** is one of the country's leading experts on children's literature, play, and development. She was honored with the Curious George Foundation Award for her work promoting literacy. Her daughter, **Stephanie Oppenheim,** is a child development expert and former corporate lawyer. She co-founded the Oppenheim Toy Portfolio with her mother soon after her first son was born. Long before she started reviewing children's books with her mother, she always enjoyed hearing her mother read to her! Joanne and Stephanie are contributors to NBC's Today show. Both live in New York City.